Tongue *Twisters*

Big Book

For Speech Clarity and Fun

By

Nilam Pathak

Anshuman Sharma

Aegis, (India) PL

Copyright

Contents

Introduction

Communication is the backbone of human development. It is responsible for thinking, generation of ideas, development of innovative solutions and sharing them with others for improvisation and enhancement. Communication also defines the success of an organization, institution, individual and even nations. The way we think and communicate our feelings to others is one of the best discovery by humanity. Without language, homo-sapiens had no chance in ruling planet earth.

For effective thinking, clarity of ideas is important. Without an organized thought process, we would be lost in a twisted mess of noise in mind. This undesirable confusion can never lead to anything productive. Once we have clarity of thought in our mind, then only it can be transferred to others.

Ideas, feelings and human thought are communicated through spoken words. The power of words delivered from the mouth can influence the hearts and minds of people. Politician, corporate brands and celebrities use them effectively. The communication language used must be simple with clarity of message delivered. For oral communication, quality of word pronunciation is as important as the ideas it contains.

A small percentage of people have clear pronunciation in oral communication. Everyone knows about its importance, but are unable to put required efforts to improve their pronunciation in their spoken language. Most people also lack the required tools and techniques to bring clarity in their speech. This book would act as one of the tools to bridge the gap to achieve exceptional oratory from basic or below average levels.

Quality in words pronunciation is appreciated by all, irrespective of the spoken language. That is necessary for fine and effective speech, which is required in all professional and personal endeavors. Many capable people fail to achieve their potential due to lack of good communication skills. An effective way to deliver the ideas and messages is a must for personal and professional success. This fact had always been correct, it is true now and it will remain valid in the distant future.

According to Oxford dictionary a 'Tongue Twister' is "a sequence of words or sounds, typically of an alliterative kind, that is difficult to pronounce quickly and correctly, as, for example, 'tie twine to three tree twigs'." We have created and collected a large list of alliteration and tongue twisters for the readers looking for speech challenges and fun.

Alliteration is used to create rhetorical impact through repetition of same sounds or the same kinds of sounds at the start of the words or in the stressed syllables, beginning either with a consonant or a vowel, in close succession. This can be used in clauses, phrases or sentences.

The phrases (alliterations and/or tongue twisters) presented in the book can be used by readers to bring clarity in their pronunciation and speech through regular intensive practice.

How to use the book

The book has been divided into two major parts. The first part deals with alliterations and tongue twisters with consonants. The second part contains tongue twisters with vowels and mixed phrases. The objective of this division is due to the fact that different people have different weaknesses in their speech. Some people have difficulties in speaking vowel words while others find consonant words as challenging. This segmentation would ease the task of finding relevant phrases for practice.

The tongue twisters presented in the book are not just for reading, instead they must be spoken aloud repeatedly, at least seven times. We will suggest repeating each of the phrases ten times, consistently without pause, with their above average spoken speed. The most important part is fluency and the clarity in pronunciation for each spoken word. You can record your practice sessions to check for the pronunciation clarity of words. Start the speaking practice of tongue twisters with slow speed and gradually increase your phrase delivery speed to your maximum limit. These exercises would be straining on the lungs, tongue, neck, and mouth. Every person has different capacity, so know your limits and care must be taken to avoid injury of any form. With constant practice, the readers would notice a gradual improvement in clarity of speech, word pronunciation and command on spoken words.

Readers can use these phrases in their unique, innovative or personalized ways to speak and practice (for their speech clarity). We will encourage them to share these ideas on social networking forums for the benefit of everyone else.

6

Consonants

The first set of tongue twisters contain phrases starting with consonants i.e. b, c, ch, d, f, g, h, j, k, l, m, n, p, q, r, s, sh, t, th, v, w, x, y, z.

B

Back of bandage with battery begin to book the bird to bury the bowl in the bathroom.

Backward of battle band-aid want the boy to behave not to bite the boots in the bush.

Busy bang's baby with black bouncy bracelet standing behind the blue boots.

Babysitter baking banjo on the beach to make the brain believe to take the blame of butter box.

Back backbone of bank rang the bell in a blanket to make brave butterfly breathe.

Bean the bar with bacon blast belt in breeze bread button.

Bad barbecue with beanbag bench blindfold to break and buy broccoli.

By the block in a bag with the bark of bear to bend the brown breakfast.

Berry the blond beast with a brush on the bridge of barn had a blast.

Bright blow baker beside baseball beat bubble by a brown bridge.

Best blue bucket basket with banjo broom beautifully balance on the bridge.

Buffalo beaver in basketball with the better ball on board border.

Ballerina between a beetle bug and borrowed bat boat put battery bandage.

Brother of balloon bib bath of the bedroom to build a body of the bouncy bracelet.

Bunny the bee avoid bicycle boil the big bad banana over the bungy bridge.

Big bow burn bone bend to beg the band in the bathtub to eat breeze bread butter.

Bob's pop-up blocker blocks Bob's pop-ups.

Bad dead bed-bugs bleed bug blood.

Bill had a billboard, Bill also had a board bill. The billboard bored Bill so Bill sold the billboard to pay for the board bill.

I can't believe that "I Can't Believe It's Not Butter!" is actually a butter that I can't believe is not butter.

If your Bob doesn't give our Bob that bob that your Bob owes our Bob, our Bob will give your Bob a bob in the eye.

Black Rock Brain Lock

My back black brake blocks are broken.

Big black bear: A big black bug bit the big black bear, but the big black bear bit the big black bug back!

Betty butter: Betty bought some butter, but the butter Betty bought was bitter, so Betty bought some better butter, and the better butter Betty bought was better than the bitter butter Betty bought before!

Biscuit mixer: I bought a bit of baking powder and baked a batch of biscuits. I brought a big basket of biscuits back to the bakery and baked a basket of big biscuits. Then I took the big basket of biscuits and the basket of big biscuits and mixed the big biscuits with the basket of biscuits that was next to the big basket and put a bunch of biscuits from the basket into a biscuit mixer and brought the basket of biscuits and the box of mixed biscuits and the biscuit mixer to the bakery and opened a tin of sardines.

Betty Botter bought some butter but, said she, the butter's bitter. If I put it in my batter, it will make my batter bitter. But a bit of better butter will make my bitter batter better. So she bought some better butter, better than the bitter butter, put it in her bitter batter, made her bitter batter better. So that was better, Betty Botter bought some better butter.

How much oil boil can a gum boil boil if a gum boil can boil oil?

Good blood, bad blood, good blood, bad blood, good blood, bad blood...

Blake's black bike's back brake bracket block broke.

The batter with the butter is the batter that is better!

Rugged rubber baby buggy bumpers.

A box of biscuits, a box of mixed biscuits, and a biscuit mixer.

One black beetle bled only black blood, the other black beetle bled blue.

The big black bug's blood ran blue.

A big black bug bit a big black bear and made the big black bear bleed blood.

To put a pipe in byte mode, type PIPE_TYPE_BYTE.

Bug's black blood, Black bug's blood.

The Smothers brothers' father's mother's brothers are the Smothers brothers' mother's father's other brothers.

Blended baby blue bug's blood blotches.

A bitter biting bittern bit a better biting bittern. And the better biting bittern bit the bitter biting bittern back. Said the bitter biting bittern to the better biting bittern "I'm a bitter biting bittern bitten back"

Broken back brake block.

You're behaving like a babbling, bumbling band of baboons.

I broke a brickbat and a brickbat broke me.

Rubber Berber Gerber™ Burger.

A big black bug bit a big black dog on his big black nose!

Bobby Bippy bought a bat. Bobby Bippy bought a ball. With his bat Bob banged the ball Banged it bump against the wall But so boldly Bobby banged it That he burst his rubber ball "Boo!" cried Bobby. Bad luck ball. Bad luck Bobby, bad luck ball Now to drown his many troubles Bobby Bippy's blowing bubbles.

Black background, brown background.

black back bat

How many berries could a bare berry carry, if a bare berry could carry berries? Well, they can't carry berries (which could make you very wary) but a bare berry carried is scary!

Red Buick, blue Buick

The big black bug bit the big black bear, but the big black bear bit the big black bug back!

As one black bug, bled blue, black blood. The other black bug bled blue.

A turbot's not a burbot, for a turbot's a butt, but a burbot's not.

Buckets of bug blood, buckets of bug blood, buckets of bug blood.

Bake big batches of bitter brown bread.

Bake big batches of the brown blueberry bread.

A black bloke's back brake-block broke.

Big black bugs bleed blue-black blood but baby black bugs bleed blue blood.

Red blood, green blood.

Busy buzzing bumble bees.

A big black bear sat on a big black bug.

A bloke's bike back brake block broke.

I bought a bit of baking powder and baked a batch of biscuits. I brought a big basket of biscuits back to the bakery and baked a basket of big biscuits. Then I took the big basket of biscuits and the basket of big biscuits and mixed the big biscuits with the basket of biscuits that was next to the big basket and put a bunch of biscuits from the basket into a biscuit mixer and brought the basket of biscuits and the box of mixed biscuits and the biscuit mixer to the bakery and opened a tin of sardines.

Ben has a bat and a ball. He likes to play with the bat and ball. Ben took his bat and played with Bob. Ben and Bob played with the bat and ball.

A big bug bit a bold bald bear and the bold bald bear bled blood badly.

Bad black bran bread.

Bake big batches of bitter brown bread.

Bake big batches of the brown blueberry bread.

Betty better butter Brad's bread.

Big Ben blew big blue bubbles.

Big black bugs bleed blue-black blood but baby black bugs bleed blue blood.

Black background, brown background.

Black Bugs Bleed Black Blood

Black bug's blood

Blake's black bike's back brake bracket block broke.

Blue bugs blood.

Brad's big black bath brush broke.

Brisk brave brigadiers brandished broad bright blades, blunderbusses, and bludgeons -- Balancing them badly.

Buckets of bug blood, buckets of bug blood, buckets of bug blood

Busy buzzing bumble bees.

The fuzzy bee buzzed the buzzy busy beehive.

Barren Beacon Beckons Bacon Baron

Good Blood, Bad Blood, Good Blood, Bad Blood, etc. Red Blood, Blue Blood, Red Blood, Blue Blood, etc.

A big black bug bit a big black bear and the big black bear bled blood.

This black bug bled blue-black blood while the other black bug bled blue.

Better Botter bought some butter. But she said this butter's bitter. If I put it in my batter. It will make my batter bitter. So, she bought some better butter. Put it in her bitter batter. And it made her bitter batter better.

When tweedle beetles battle. With paddles in a puddle. They call it a tweedle beetle puddle paddle battle.

Bobby Bibby bought a bat. Bobby Bibby bought a ball. With his bat, Bob banged the ball. Banged it bumps against the wall. But so badly Bobby banged it. That he burst his rubber ball. Boo! Cried. Bobby, Bad luck, the ball! Bad luck, Bobby, Bad Luck ball. Now to drown his many troubles. Bobby Bibby's blowing bubbles.

Black Bart was a smart marksman.

A box of biscuits. A box of mixed biscuits. And a biscuit mixer.

Betty Botter bought some butter, "But," she said, "this butter's bitter. If I bake this bitter butter, It will make my batter bitter. But a bit of better butter - That would make my batter better." So, she bought a bit of butter, Better than her bitter butter, And she baked it in her batter, And the batter was not bitter. So that was better Betty Botter, Bought a bit of better butter. Betty and Bob brought back blue balloons from the big bazaar. A big black bug bit a big black bear made the big black bear bleed blood.

Black bug's blood. The blue bluebird blinks. The bootblack bought the black boot back. A box of biscuits, a batch of mixed biscuits. Brad's big black bath brush broke.

Once upon a barren moor. There dwelt a bear, also a boar, The bear could not bear the boar, The bear thought the boar was a bore. At last the bear could bear no more That boar that bored him on the moor. And so one morning he bored the boar- That boar will bore no more!

A big bug bit a bold bald bear and the bold bald bear bled blood badly. Bad black bran bread. Big Ben blew big blue bubbles. The fuzzy bee buzzed the buzzy busy beehive. Blue bugs blood.

I bought a box of biscuits, a box of mixed biscuits, and a biscuit mixer.

Bill had a billboard. Bill also had a board bill. The board bill bored Bill. So Bill sold his billboard and paid his board bill. Then the board bill. No longer bored Bill. But though he had no board bill. Neither did he have his billboard!

Little Bill, sit still. Will you sit still, little Bill? If you sit still, little Bill, Jimmy Nill will bring you to a big hill.

C

Cranky cluck cottage crumbles on computer cabin for clasp care.

Cotton clump cable crash crumbly on concerns of the careful class copter.

Caramel caboose clatter carefully crawled below couch with clunk crunch.

Carnival clunky crackle claw cough crazy on a crunchy cone.

Confetti could create clay clutter crush on cage carpet.

Confused coach counts creaky crust to clean carrot cake.

Connect clear counter calendar to cry and carry coal cream counter.

Contact country creek crystal with clench cart calf coat.

California click cartwheel contain creep cocoa cub couple.

Continue carbon creepy cliff cover coconut call cube to contact coal.

Calm cow cartoon crew climb contrast cubby code.

Control cozy crib cuckoo coin climber camera case.

Cook cucumber with crab coke to cling cricket cash at camp.

Crabby crinkle cuddle cookie cast cold clip can in the canister.

Cool crisp candy cloak collar in castle cuddled to crack camera.

Crocodile cracker cop collects clock cup and a candle for the cat.

Crackling cupcake crook copy color to catch clomp cane.

Crooked crackly curb cord went close to colt caterpillar on canoe.

Corn crop cradle cured but caught closed comb cap with creek crystal.

Corner craft cloth with cross curl come to cape cave.

Correct clothe comfort cram on crouch curtain with capital clack.

Common cramp clothes with crow curves capture clam caterpillar.

Compare clank cramped cushion in castle car crowd near the high cotton cloud.

Common card club clap and complain to cranking crumb cat on the cot.

What's a synonym for cinnamon or is cinnamon synonym-less?

Clam cream can: How can a clam cram in a clean cream can?

Can you can a can: Can you can a can as a canner can can a can?

Copyright: When you write copy you have the right to copyright the copy you write.

Good cook: How many cookies could a good cook cook. If a good cook could cook cookies? A good cook could cook as many cookies as a good cook who could cook cookies.

How many cans?: How many cans can a cannibal nibble, if a cannibal can nibble cans? As many cans as a cannibal can nibble if a cannibal can nibble cans.

Spell Chicago: Chicken in the car and the car can go, that is the way you spell Chicago.

If Stu chews shoes, should Stu choose the shoes he chews?

Craig Quinn's quick trip to Crabtree Creek.

Mrs. Hunt had a country cut front in the front of her country cut petticoat.

Clowns grow glowing crowns.

A proper cup of coffee from a proper copper coffee pot.

I would if I could, and if I couldn't, how could I? You couldn't unless you could, could you?

How many cans can a canner can if a canner can can cans? A canner can can as many cans as a canner can if a canner can can cans.

A quick-witted cricket critic.

The cat crept into the crypt, crapped and crept out.

Certified certificates from certified certificate certifiers.

Crash Quiche Course.

Give papa a cup of proper coffee in a copper coffee cup.

Six Czech cricket critics.

How much cash could a sasquatch stash if a sasquatch could stash cash?

A cunning young canner from Canning. Once observed to his granny, "A canner can can a lot of things gran, But a canner can't can a can, can he?"

Click, clap, pluck, ...

A canner exceedingly canny, One morning remarked to his granny, A canner can can, Anything that he can, But a canner can't can a can; can he?

chip shop chips

Cracker rapper, cracker rapper, cracker rapper, ...

Cook "Cookie" Turk took Kookie Kirk a turkey cookie.

A synonym for cinnamon is a cinnamon synonym.

How can a clam cram in a clean cream can?

Can you can a can as a canner can can a can?

You cuss, I cuss, we all cuss, for asparagus!

Clean clams crammed in clean cans.

Celibate celebrant, celibate celebrant, celibate celebrant, ...

How many cookies could a good cook cook If a good cook could cook cookies? A good cook could cook as many cookies as a good cook who could cook cookies.

How many cans can a cannibal nibble if a cannibal can nibble cans? As many cans as a cannibal can nibble if a cannibal can nibble cans.

Snap Crackle pop, Snap Crackle pop, Snap Crackle pop

Six slimy snails sailed silently.

How much caramel can a canny cannonball cram in a camel if a canny cannonball can cram caramel in a camel?

I'll chew and chew until my jaws drop.

Chester Cheetah chews a chunk of cheap cheddar cheese.

If you're keen on stunning kites and cunning stunts, buy a cunning stunning stunt kite.

If you can't can any candy can, how many candy cans can a candy canner can if he can can candy cans?

It's not the cough that carries you off, it's the coffin they carry you off in!

Knife and a fork bottle and a cork that is the way you spell New York. Chicken in the car and the car can go, that is the way you spell Chicago.

If colored caterpillars could change their colors constantly could they keep their colored coat colored properly?

When you write copy you have the right to copyright the copy you write if the copy is right. If however, your copy falls over, you must write your copy. If you write religious services you write rite and have the right to copyright the rite you write.

Very conservative people write right to copy and have the right to copyright the right copy they write. A right wing cleric would write right rite and has the right to copyright the right rite he has the right to write. His editor has the job of making the right rite copy right before the copyright can be right.

The cat and cow had tea one day. The cow had a cold cake with hay. The cat cut some cake and let out a shout. My cake is in my tea and I can't get it out.

A cup of proper coffee in a copper coffee cup.

A cupcake cook in a cupcake cook's cap cooks cupcakes.

Ape Cakes, Grape Cakes.

Catch a can canner canning a can as he does the cancan, and you've caught a can-canning can-canning can canner!

Cheap sheep soup.

Chocolate chip cookies in a copper coffee cup.

Cinnamon aluminum linoleum.

Clean clams crammed in clean cans.

Crisp crust crackles.

Cuthbert's cufflinks.

How much can can a cannibal nibble if a cannibal can nibble can?

If you must cross a course cross cow across a crowded cow crossing, cross the cross coarse cow across the crowded cow crossing carefully.

Top chopstick shops stock top chopsticks.

Cedar shingles should be shaved and saved.

A cheap ship trip.

Chop shops stock chops.

Cows graze in groves on grass which grows in grooves in groves.

Crisp crusts crackle crunchily.

The crow flew over the river with a lump of raw liver.

A proper cup of coffee from a proper copper coffee pot.

Catch a can canner canning a can as he does the cancan, and you've caught a can-canning can-canning can canner!

Clams crammed in clean cans.

How much can can a cannibal nibble if a cannibal can nibble can?

Top chopstick shops stock top chopsticks.

Cuthbert's cufflinks.

A cupcake cook in a cupcake cook's cap cooks cupcakes.

Crisp crust crackles.

Chocolate chip cookies in a copper coffee cup.

Ape Cakes, Grape Cakes.

Cinnamon aluminum linoleum.

If you must cross a course cross cow across a crowded cow crossing, cross the cross coarse cow across the crowded cow crossing carefully.

Cheap sheep soup.

A cup of proper coffee in a copper coffee cup.

CH

Chew cold chime chain chocolate on a cot with chow chat but clean cat cheek.

Camera choice of chick chub chimney play cheap cool checkers on code chair.

Chimp count chicken chooses chuck coin to cheer chalk climber chat.

Child cube chin chops crunchy cheese to change chase of confused chicken.

Choppy chug chased cold cherry chili collar chip to charge crisp cheap chain.

Chum chipmunk chill with cookie and chopstick play chess on charm castle chat.

Chilly chunk with cash chirp check chart on coconut chest chore.

How much wood could Chuck Woods' woodchuck chuck if Chuck Woods' woodchuck could and would chuck wood? If Chuck Woods' woodchuck could and would chuck wood, how much wood could and would Chuck Woods' woodchuck chuck? Chuck Woods' woodchuck would chuck, he would, as much as he could, and chuck as much wood as any

woodchuck would if a woodchuck could and would chuck wood.

Swatch watch

If a dog chews shoes, whose shoes does he choose?

D

Dad digs dirty dish with donkey duck dancing in drawn dent drawer in the dawn.

Daily dug dentist day starts in distance digging dark door drawing the dress.

Dead desert dime distracts dull dot dream in dairy to draw dog dice.

Deaf Daisy dines double dessert to dive in dump dress with the dentist.

Dear Dalmatian divide and destroy dresser dove with ding and dust.

Detective David had dinner and dance down in December for daily drill.

Diamond dinosaur in downstairs dock drip on dandelion deck to distract donkey.

Doctor Danger decorates diaper to drag drive with dip drum to dance decently.

Dare dog drop dice deep to distract the dragon.

Dirty dragonfly drove deer in dark to dig dictionary with the doll.

Disagree defend die with a dart to drain dollar and destroy drum.

Dry dolphin delivers different drama at distance to get dash disc.

Domino daughter in disguise draw difficult dryer from dinosaur den.

Diamond on deck divide donkey and deer on dessert with dirty dog dancing.

Triple Dickle a strong drink.

Double bubble gum, bubbles double.

Dust is a disk's worst enemy.

How much dew does a dewdrop drop. If dewdrops do drop dew? They do drop, they do. As do dewdrops drop. If dewdrops do drop dew.

When a doctor doctors a doctor, does the doctor doing the doctoring doctor as the doctor being doctored wants to be doctored or does the doctor doing the doctoring doctor as he wants to doctor?

What to do to die today at a minute or two to two. A terribly difficult thing to say and a harder thing to do. A dragon will come and beat his drum Ra-ta-ta-ta-ta-ta-ta-too at a minute or two to two today. At a minute or two to two.

How much dough would Bob Dole dole if Bob Dole could dole dough? Bob Dole would dole as much dough as Bob Dole could dole if Bob Dole could dole dough.

Did Doug dig Dick's garden or did Dick dig Doug's garden?

Ken Dodd's dad's dog 's dead.

One Double Dozen Double Damask Dinner Napkins.

He wanted to desert his dessert in the desert!

Dick had a dog, the dog dug, the dog dug deep, how deep did Dick's dog dig? Dick had a duck, the duck dived, the duck dived deep, how deep did Dick's duck dive? Dick's duck dived as deep as Dick's dog dug!

M. R. Ducks M.R. not Ducks O. S. M. R. L. I'll B. M. R. Ducks!

How many ducks could a duck duct-tape if a duck could duct-tape ducks?

Deer, deer, oh dear, oh dear, your career as a deer is over here no, no, oh no, although your career as a Pushtun's begun.

Darn dawn dog gone!

It dawned on Don at dawn.

Darla's dollars.

Doctor doctoring: When a doctor doctors a doctor, does the doctor doing the doctoring doctor as the doctor being

doctored wants to be doctored or does the doctor doing the doctoring doctor as he wants to doctor?

When a doctor falls ill another doctor doctor's the doctor. Does the doctor doctoring the doctor doctor the doctor in his own way or does the doctor doctoring the doctor doctors the doctor in the doctor's way?

Dan and Deb went to a ball. They took their dog and doll with them. The dog got lost in the fog. And Dan dropped the doll in the bog.

A dozen dim ding-dongs.

Did Dick Pickens prick his pinkie pickling cheap cling peaches in an inch of Pinch or framing his famed French finch photos?

Does this shop sport short socks with spots?

Don't pamper damp scamp tramps that camp under ramp lamps.

Don't spring on the inner-spring this spring or there will be an offspring next spring.

Double bubble gum, bubbles double.

Dr. Johnson and Mr. Johnson, after great consideration, came to the conclusion that the Indian nation beyond the Indian Ocean is back in education because the chief occupation is cultivation.

Dust is a disk's worst enemy.

How much dew would a dewdrop drop if a dewdrop did drop dew?

When a doctor gets sick and another doctor doctors him, does the doctor doing the doctoring have to doctor the doctor the way the doctor being doctored wants to be doctored, or does the doctor doing the doctoring of the doctor doctor the doctor as he wants to do the doctoring?

A dozen dim ding-dongs.

How much dew would a dewdrop drop if a dewdrop did drop dew?

F

Freeze fat flag floss to face frozen fidget fish's flash message.

Father fact on field forget fruit freezer with flour flake, frog feet, flippers, and swim fins.

Forgive fifty factory French flakes favor fruity flow.

Fry flame flower forgot favorite fight to fail and frustrate.

Fear figure flap fluff to fork fair frequent fry.

Fairy fresh fudge play feast flute to fill flash fort.

Filthy fly with fake forth feather fall flat on fuel first Friday.

Fortune fridge was full in February with fresh flavor fudge.

Forward flying final flea fried false fed for fun.

Funny friend found foam fame to find flee fee.

Fine fur feed fog fountain fright fleece family to find the flash flute.

Famous four fingers in foil feel furious flick on the fringe.

Fourth frisbee furniture flies fold fan feeling finish.

Fancy fins feet of flying fox follow frisky furry.

Fantastic fragile frizz food flip factory fire felt freeze further.

Flipper the fussy fool fought first far from frame felt frizzy.

Frank the frog flirt with fuzz the fish forty feet from the farm.

Flit farmer foot float from fence to fray fist float.

Fred the fit flock flew farther to follow frosting festival.

Free fashion fever fix frothy force of fake French freezer.

Fancy flop factory in forest frown freely to fly fast past fewer than five favorite forces.

They hatch fish at the state fish hatchery and sell hatched fish to the fish stick factory.

Farrell's features fabulous food 'n' fantastic fountain fantasies for frolicking, fun-filled festive families.

Frank's fisher fishes on Friday for Frank's Friday fresh fried fish-fest.

If a fella met a fella in a field of fitches. Can a fella tell a fella where a fella itches?

I feel a feel a funny feel a funny feel feel I, If I feel a funny feel a funny feel feel I.

Faith's face cloth, Faith's face cloth, Faith's face cloth, ...

Old lady Hunt had a cuzzy Funt not a cuzzy Funt but a Hunt Funt cuzzy.

Fresh fish and fried prawns.

Friskies frisbee.

Four furious friends: Four furious friends fought for the phone.

There was a fisherman named Fisher who fished for some fish in a fissure. Till a fish with a grin, pulled the fisherman in. Now they're fishing the fissure for Fisher.

Through three cheese trees three free fleas flew. While these fleas flew, freezy breeze blew. Freezy breeze made these three trees freeze. Freezy trees made these trees' cheese freeze. That's what made these three free fleas sneeze.

Four furious friends fought for the phone.

Fresh French fried fly fritters

East Fife Four, Forfar Five

Five frantic frogs fled from fifty fierce fishes.

One smart fellow, he felt smart. Two smart fellows, they felt smart. Three smart fellows, they felt smart. Four smart

fellows, they felt smart. Five smart fellows, they felt smart. Six smart fellows, they felt smart.

Five fuzzy French frogs Frolicked through the fields in France.

A fly and flea flew into a flue, said the fly to the flea 'what shall we do?' 'let us fly' said the flea said the fly 'shall we flee' so they flew through a flaw in the flue.

Fresh fried fish, Fish fresh fried, Fried fish fresh, Fish fried fresh.

Freshly fried fresh flesh.

A flea and a fly in a flue were imprisoned. So what could they do? Said the fly, "Let us flee". Said the flea, "Let us fly". So they flew through a flaw in the flue.

Five fat friars frying flatfish.

Flies fly but a fly flies.

Federal Express is now called FedEx. When I retire I'll be a FedEx ex. But if I'm an officer when I retire, I'll be an ex Fedex Exec. Then after a divorce, my ex-wife will be an ex FedEx exec's ex. If I rejoin FedEx in time, I'd be an ex-ex FedEx exec. When we remarry, my wife will be an ex-ex FedEx exec's ex.

Furnish Freddie's nursery with forty-four furry Furby Beanie Babies.

Freddy is ready to roast red roaches. Ready for Freddy's roasted red roaches?

Of all the felt I ever felt I never felt felt that felt like that felt felt.

The Final Fixing of the Foolish Fugitive

Feeling footloose, fancy-free and frisky, this feather-brained fellow finagled his fond father into forking over his fortune. Forthwith, he fled for foreign fields and frittered his farthings feasting fabulously with fair-weather friends. Finally, fleeced by those folly-filled

fellows and facing famine, he found himself a feed-flinger in a filthy farm-lot. He fain would have filled his frame with foraged food from fodder fragments.

"Fooey! My father's flunkies fare far fancier," the frazzled fugitive fumed feverishly, frankly facing the fact.

Frustrated from failure and filled with forebodings, he fled for his family. Falling at his father's feet, he floundered forlornly. "Father, I have flunked and fruitlessly forfeited further family favors . . ."

But the faithful father, forestalling further flinching, frantically flagged his flunkies to fetch forth the finest fatling and fix a feast.

But the fugitive's fault-finding frater, faithfully farming his father's fields for free, frowned at this fickle forgiveness of former falderal. His fury flashed, but fussing was futile.

His foresighted father figured, "Such filial fidelity is fine, but what forbids fervent festivities? The fugitive is found! Unfurl the flags! With fanfare flaring, let fun, frolic, and

frivolity flow freely, former failures are forgotten and folly is forsaken."

Forgiveness forms a firm foundation for future fortitude.

Fifi the fish had a fine hat with four feathers. Felix the fox took out the feathers. Fifi the fish was very angry with Felix. You foolish fellow! Now my fine hat is in a mess.

Fat frogs flying past fast.

Five fat friars frying flatfish.

Five frantic frogs fled from fifty fierce fishes.

Five fuzzy French frogs Frolicked through the fields in France.

Flee from fog to fight flu fast!

Flies fly but a fly flies.

Four furious friends fought for the phone.

Fred fed Ted bread, and Ted fed Fred bread.

Fresh French fried fly fritters

Freshly fried fresh flesh.

Freshly-fried flying fish.

Friendly Frank flips fine flapjacks.

Frogfeet, flippers, swimfins.

A fat-free fruit float.

False Frank fled Flo Friday.

Few free fruit flies fly from flames.

Four free-flow pipes flow freely.

Fran feeds fish fresh fish food.

Freckle-faced Freddie fidgets.

I'm not a fig plucker nor a fig plucker's son, but I'll pluck your fig's 'til the fig plucker comes.

The fickle finger of fate flips fat frogs flat.

Try fat flat flounders.

Fat frogs flying past fast.

Flee from fog to fight flu fast!

Fred fed Ted bread, and Ted fed Fred bread.

Freshly fried flying fish, freshly fried flesh.

Friendly Frank flips fine flapjacks.

Freckle-faced Freddie fidgets.

The fickle finger of fate flips fat frogs flat.

Try fat flat flounders.

Fran feeds fish fresh fish food.

Few free fruit flies fly from flames.

I'm not a fig plucker nor a fig plucker's son, but I'll pluck your fig's 'til the fig plucker comes.

False Frank fled Flo Friday.

Four free-flow pipes flow freely.

A fat-free fruit float.

A flea and a fly in a flue. Were imprisoned, so what could they do? Said the flea "Let us fly!" Said the fly "Let us flee!!" So they flew through a flaw in the flue.

Fuzzy Wuzzy was a bear. Fuzzy Wuzzy had no hair. Fuzzy Wuzzy wasn't fuzzy, was he?

One smart fellow, he felt smart. Two smart fellows, they felt smart. Three smart fellows, they felt smart. Four smart fellows, they felt smart. Five smart fellows, they felt smart. Six smart fellows, they felt smart. Seven smart fellows, they felt smart. Eight smart fellows, they felt smart. Nine smart fellows, they felt smart. Ten smart fellows, they felt smart!

G

Green grumble gun gobble green grade to get game.

Garbage ghost with glitter gold grain grew gutter guard.

Grand globe golf guessed the gift in the garden with a grin.

Gloomy grandmother grinds garlic gazing the guest with a giggle.

Good glove gives grape to guide the ground gas.

Glow grass group glad goose on guilt gate.

Grateful gorilla in grove gather glue for guitar glare.

Gravy growl gull gave the glad glittering gown a go.

Grab gray grown gum to gear gleam goat eating green grass.

Grip glue, grip glue, grip glue, ...

I gratefully gazed at the gracefully grazing gazelles.

You name it, we claim it. If we can't get it, we'll send you to get it. If we can't send you to get it, forget it. Who's got it, if we didn't get it?

Great Gate Crasher.

Grandma Gabby Grammer grabbed a gram of gummy goulash. If Grandma Gabby Grammer grabbed a gram of gummy goulash. How many grams of gummy goulash did Grandma Gabby Grammer grab?

Green glass globes: Green glass globes glow greenly.

Gobbling gargoyles gobbled gobbling goblins.

How much ground would a groundhog hog if a groundhog could hog ground? A groundhog would hog all the ground he could hog if a groundhog could hog ground.

Green glass globes glow greenly.

The great Greek grape growers grow great Greek grapes.

A gazillion gigantic grapes gushed gradually giving gophers gooey guts.

How much ground could a groundhog grind if a groundhog could grind ground?

As he gobbled the cakes on his plate, the greedy ape said as he ate, the greener green grapes are, the keener keen apes are to gobble green grape cakes, they're great!

Crush grapes, grapes crush, crush grapes.

Great gray goats.

Greek grapes.

Gus goes by Blue Goose bus.

Cows graze in droves on grass that grows on grooves in groves.

Gale's great glass globe glows green.

Blue glue gun, green glue gun.

My Friend Gladys. Oh, the sadness of her sadness when she's sad. Oh, the gladness of her gladness when she's glad. But the sadness of her sadness and the gladness of her gladness are nothing like her madness when she's mad!

If you go for a gopher a gopher will go for a gopher hole.

Three grey geese. In a green field grazing, Grey were the geese. And green was the grazing.

Giddy kiddy goat, Giddy kiddy goat. Giddy, giddy, giddy, giddy, giddy, kiddy goat.

Greg the goat had a party in his garden. Gigi the goose got her guitar and sat down to play. Gigi the goose let out a cry. There's gum on my guitar and I don't know why!

Cows graze in droves on grass that grows on grooves in groves.

Gale's great glass globe glows green.

Gertie's great-grandma grew aghast at Gertie's grammar.

Girl gargoyle, guy gargoyle.

Give Mr. Snipa's wife's knife a swipe.

Give papa a cup of proper coffee in a copper coffee cup.

Gobbling gargoyles gobbled gobbling goblins.

Good blood, bad blood.

Great gray goats

Greek grapes.

Green glass globes glow greenly.

Gus goes by Blue Goose bus.

H

Hanging heap hive honk hospital as a hobby to hang heavy hornet.

Heady had a hot hanger to hide hood hair of high hero of Hollywood.

Hungry hippy had half happy heart got hiccup to hunt hoof hot-dog.

Hurry, hide hog hook in hotel hall from hard heat on the hill.

Heavy harp holds high in hoop hound could hurt Halloween holiday.

Hush hedgehog in the house had ham hat with hole said hooray.

Hope to hop with the heel on holiday hill with hamburger to hoot.

How to hate hollow hop howl which has hammer height.

I hope to hug hawk helicopter at hamster home on the holiday.

Helena had a huge horn hippopotamus with a heavy hand.

45

Handcuffed hay hum hello in hat got help to hire and hasten to the hidden hornet.

Human horse with hen head handle history homework.

Handy honey hose hit her health in a hundred happening ways.

Helipad hears helicopter hooting hooray with hiccup to howl history homework.

In 'Hertford, 'Hereford and 'Hampshire, 'hurricanes 'hardly Hever 'happen.

Hassock hassock, black spotted hassock. Black spot on a black back of a black spotted hassock.

John, where Peter had had "had had", had had "had"; "had had" had had his master's approval.

John, where 'Molly had' had "had", 'had' had "had had". "Had had " and 'had' had the teacher's approval.

Miss Smith's fish-sauce shop seldom sells shellfish.

Larry Hurley, a burly squirrel hurler, hurled a furry squirrel through a curly grill.

If a Hottentot taught a Hottentot tot to talk ere the tot could totter, ought the Hottentot tot be taught to say ought or naught or what ought to be taught 'er?

Hitchcock Hawk Watch Spots Record Raptors.

If a Hottentot tot taught a Hottentot tot to talk before the tot would totter, ought the Hottentot tot be taught to say ought, or naught, or what ought to be taught the Hottentot tot? If to hoot and to toot a Hottentot tot be taught by a Hottentot tutor, should the tutor get hot if the Hottentot tot hoots and toots at the Hottentot tutor?

In Hertford, Hereford, and Hampshire hurricanes hardly ever happen.

Hercules, a hardy hunter, hunted a hare in the Hampshire Hills. Hit him on the head with a hard, hard hammer and he howled horribly!

Hulk Hawk is hulking the hawk, Hawk Hulk is hawking Hulk ... Hawk hugs the hedgehog.

Helen's husband hates hot tea. Henry's horse has hurt his hoof in a hole while hunting.

The horse and the hippo hopped hand in hand. Henry the horse and Harry the hippo had a lot of fun. They got tired and huffed and puffed as they sat in the sun.

Hassock hassock, black spotted hassock. Black spot on a black back of a black spotted hassock.

He threw three balls.

He threw three free throws.

Hiccup teacup!

Higgledy-Piggedly!

Hi-Tech Traveling Tractor Trailor Truck Tracker

How can a clam cram in a clean cream can?

How many berries could a bare berry carry,

How many cans can a canner can if a canner can can cans? A canner can can as many cans as a canner can if a canner can can cans.

How many moose might a mini-mouse move if a mini-mouse might move moose?

How many sheets could a sheet slitter slit if a sheet slitter could slit sheets?

How many yaks could a yak pack pack if a yak pack could pack yaks?

How much caramel can a canny cannonball cram in a camel if a canny cannonball can cram caramel in a camel?

How much ground could a groundhog grind if a groundhog could grind ground?

How much oil boil can a gum boil boil if a gum boil can boil oil?

How much pot, could a pot roast roast if a pot roast could roast pot.

The hare's ear heard ere the hare heeded.

Higgledy-Piggedly!

The hare's ear heard ere the hare heeded.

Hiccup teacup!

A haddock! A haddock! A black-spotted haddock! A black spot. On the black back. Of a black-spotted haddock!

J

Jack the judge jiggle jellybean in January jungle to jab joke.

Jim the junior jellyfish juggle jolly with a jingle in a jar.

Junk jaw jacket of jerk jot gel to ring a bell.

Jagged journey jitter just jumbles jazzy jet.

Jealous jaguar jot July jigsaw for the joy of jewel.

Joyful jumbo jacks jog jail in a jeep with jewelry.

Jubilant jiffy join jump jelly jello jam.

Jangle jelly Judge jig joint in June.

Just a joke. Julius was jealous. Jane, Jim, and George Jones. John put the orange juice into the fridge.

Jerry the joker juggled jars in the jungle while eating his jam and bread. The jars came tumbling down in the jumble. Now Jerry has a lump on his head.

Jack the jailbird jacked a jeep.

Judicial system.

June sheep sleep soundly.

Jack the jailbird jacked a jeep.

Our Joe wants to know if your Joe will lend, our Joe you Joe's banjo. If your Joe won't lend us. Joe your Joe's banjo our Joe won't lend your Joe our Joe's banjo when our Joe has a banjo!

A gentle judge judges justly.

June sheep sleep soundly.

Judicial system.

K

Kind kangaroo kick kite keeper keyboard keyhole.

Karate Kindergarten kitten kid keeps Kent kilobyte.

Kleenex kennel kin keeps king kidney.

Kil has been key is keen to kiss keyboard kit.

Little Mike left his bike like Tike at Spike's.

Ken can ken that Ken's kin can ken Ken's kin's ken.

Kitty the kitten has been naughty today. She locked the kangaroo in the kitchen and hid the key. Now she's flying Kevin the koala's kite- oh dear me!

A knapsack strap.

Keenly cleaning copper kettles.

Kinky kite kits.

Kiss her quick, kiss her quicker, kiss her quickest!

Come kick six sticks quick.

Kanta is a Masai girl, she can tie a tie and untie a tie if Kanta can tie a tie and untie a tie, why can't I tie a tie and untie a tie?

Ken Dodd's dad's dog 's dead.

Knapsack strap.

Knife and a fork bottle and a cork

Kris Kringle carefully crunched on candy canes.

Kinky kite kits.

A knapsack strap.

Keenly cleaning copper kettles.

Come kick six sticks quick.

Kiss her quick, kiss her quicker, kiss her quickest!

L

·

Lower lollipop lead label lends litter lie language.

Labor leader loyal little life lift lone lantern length.

Live leaf lonely luck lifts lace lens lap.

Long large leopard liver leak log lace on luggage.

Living leprechaun-like leap lasagna with lullaby lad lovely look.

Lilly the laser lizard loom lumber ladder to learn less.

Lucy the last lady at London lower leash limb lesson to llama loop lump.

Loose leather ladybug let loose load lime at-least.

Laundry lair limp loaf loot leave a letter on the ledge.

Lose line lobster lettuce led lake laugh.

Local ledge link label level lamb launch.

Lame lava license of lock lion left lotion.

Loud lamp legend lick locket law lemon lips.

Logan loves licorice lay legs list on lodge land.

Lane lazy lemon listens to log low lid of ladybug luggage.

Luke Luck likes lakes. Luke's duck likes lakes. Luke Luck licks lakes. Luck's duck licks lakes. Duck takes licks in lakes Luke Luck likes. Luke Luck takes licks in lakes duck likes.

On a lazy laser raiser lies a laser ray eraser.

Love's a feeling you feel when you feel, you're going to feel the feeling you've never felt before.

A lump of red leather, a red leather lump.

If you stick a stock of liquor in your locker it is slick to stick a lock upon your stock or some joker who is slicker is going to trick you of your liquor if you fail to lock your liquor with a lock.

Red leather, yellow leather, ...

Red lorry, yellow lorry.

The little red lorry went down Limuru road.

Lady Luck dislikes losers.

Lucid Lou slued lose the sluice that slew the slough.

Lenny Lou leopard led leprechauns leaping like lemmings.

loyal royal lawyer.

Lester the lion likes the little lamb. But the lamb is scared of him. Lester will gobble him up like a big lollipop. And they lick his lips with a grin.

Larry Hurley, a burly squirrel hurler, hurled a furry squirrel through a curly grill.

Larry sent the latter a letter later.

Lesser leather never weathered lesser wetter weather.

Lesser leather never weathered wetter weather better.

Lily ladles little Letty's lentil soup.

Lisa laughed listlessly.

Listen to the local yokel yodel.

Literally literary.

Little Mike left his bike like Tike at Spike's.

Lonely lowland llamas are ladylike.

Lovely lemon liniment.

Love's a feeling you feel when you feel you're going to feel the feeling you've never felt before.

Red leather! Yellow leather!

Yellow lorry, blue lorry.

Lonely lowland llamas are ladylike.

Lisa laughed listlessly.

Larry sent the latter a letter later.

Red leather! Yellow leather!

Lesser leather never weathered lesser wetter weather.

Yellow lorry, blue lorry.

If you stick a stock of liquor in your locker, it is slick to put a lock upon your stock. For some joker who is quicker will rob you of your liquor, if you fail to lock your liquor with a lock.

M

Mummy mix most macaroni with mask medicine in mall microwave.

Medium middle mast motel munch moat of mama machine.

Master muscle man meets moth mad model in midnight.

Mane mother made might melon from mold on the mat at the museum.

Mom mush motor matches the mild melt magazine manager.

Magic mango member mound mushroom materials on market mile.

Memorize magnet mountain math with music, milk, and manners.

Mattress memory must magnify money by many millions for the master mouse.

May monkey with mouth mustache use men to make glass map.

Mustard monster mayor moves mine mend marble to the maid.

My mini mouth mow march mail menu in the maze.

Martial moon met me on the moon to the mint mailbox with a meow.

Main mermaid marks me moon moose muck minute on meadow mud.

Major mirror marries mop mud for mini marker meal on Monday.

More muffin means market mess to make mere melon.

Messy morning mission measure to make monster monkey marry.

Metal meat marshmallow mistake mule for mosquito.

Mash male microphone mumble mitten moss to mark magic medal.

Mary Mac's mother's making Mary Mac marry me. My mother's making me marry Mary Mac. Will I always be so Merry when Mary's taking care of me?

Will I always be so merry when I marry Mary Mac?

Roofs of mushrooms rarely mush too much.

Mo mi mo me send me a toe, Me me mo mi get me a mole, Mo mi mo me send me a toe, Fe me mo mi get me a mole, Mister Kister feet so sweet, Mister Kister where will I eat !?

Mommy made me eat my M&Ms.

Mummies make money.

There was a minimum of cinnamon in the aluminum pan.

Can you imagine an imaginary menagerie manager imagining managing an imaginary menagerie?

Meter maid Mary married manly Matthew Marcus Mayo, a moody male mailman moving mostly metered mail.

Moses supposes his toeses are roses, but Moses supposes erroneously. For Moses, he knowses his toeses aren't roses, as Moses supposes his toeses to be.

My mommy makes me muffins on Mondays.

Imagine, imagining, an imaginary imaginary imaginary menagerie manager, imagining imagining imagining an imaginary imaginary imaginary menagerie.

Mumbling, bumbling. Bumbling, mumbling.

Mudbug, mudbug, mudbug, ...

A maid named Lady Marmalade made mainly lard and lemonade. M'lady lamely never made a well-named, labeled marmalade.

Midget beget minute, midget beget minute, midget begets minute, ...

Mary Mac: Mary Mac's mother's making Mary Mac marry me. My mother's making me marry Mary Mac. Will I always be so Merry when Mary's taking care of me? Will I always be so merry when I marry Mary Mac?

Maggie the magpie has a magic mop. It mops up any mess in a minute. So when Matt the monkey split his mango milkshake. Maggie used the mop on her mat to clean it.

A missing mixture measure.

Mallory's hourly salary.

Many an anemone sees an enemy anemone.

Miss Smith lisps as she talks and lists as she walks.

Miss Smith's fish-sauce shop seldom sells shellfish.

Mix, Miss Mix!

Mommy made me eat my M&Ms.

Moose noshing much mush.

Mr. Tongue Twister tried to train his tongue to twist and turn, and twit and twat, to learn the letter, T.

Mrs. Hunt had a country cut front in the front of her country cut petticoat.

Mrs. Smith's Fish Sauce Shop.

Many mashed mushrooms.

Mummies make money.

Why may we melee, when we may waylay?

Imagine an imaginary menagerie manager, imagining managing an imaginary menagerie.

She stood upon the balcony, inimically mimicking him, hiccupping while amicably welcoming him in.

Any noise annoys an oyster, but a noisy noise annoys an oyster most.

You know New York, you need New York. You know you need unique New York.

My dame hath a lame tame crane, My dame hath a crane that is lame.

Miss Smith lisps as she talks and lists as she walks.

I miss my Swiss Miss. My Swiss Miss misses me.

A missing mixture measures.

Why may we melee, when we may waylay?

N

Nice natural necklace of the north now nets nobody's nail.

Number nose nice necktie of niece never name nature as nasty.

New naughty nurse needs noise to not nap in the night.

Navy news nightmare need napkin note to needle none.

Near neighbor of narrow nine-note nonsense of newspaper nothing.

Nasty neat neon notices no next noodle.

Noble nation nibble nest neck on November noon.

If you notice this notice, you will notice that this notice is not worth noticing.

Nat the bat swat at Matt the gnat.

No nose knows the goose like a gnome's nose knows.

What noise annoys an oyster most? A noisy noise annoys an oyster most.

A nurse anesthetist unearthed a nest.

A noise annoys an oyster, but a noisy noise annoys an oyster more!

No need to light a night-light on a light night like tonight.

What noise annoys a noisy oyster? Any noise annoys a noisy oyster, but a noisy noise annoys a noisy oyster most!

Nine nice night nurses nursing nicely.

It's a nice night for a white rice fight.

A noisy noise annoys an oyster.

Naughty Ned poked his nanny with a needle one night. She put a napkin on her neck and ran to the nurse. Nurse Nora put a plaster on Nanny's neck. Now wasn't that naughty of naughty Ned?

Nick knits Nixon's knickers.

Nine nice night nymphs.

Nine nimble noblemen nibbled nuts

Norse myths.

A noisy noise annoys an oyster.

Nat the bat swat at Matt the gnat.

National Sheep-shire Sheep Association.

Near an ear, a nearer ear, a nearly eerie ear.

Never trouble about trouble until trouble troubles you!

Nine nice night nurses nursing nicely.

No need to light a night light on a light night like tonight.

Nothing is worth thousands of deaths.

Nine nice night nurses nursing nicely.

Nick knits Nixon's knickers.

Nine nimble noblemen nibbled nuts.

A noisy noise annoys an oyster.

Norse myths. Nine nice night nymphs.

P

Parent picnic plan pours poker progress to peck pace.

Picture pedal polar plane pout promise on pack park.

Power pad pear on power planet property peek parrot pie.

Plant pole piece protects peel part to practice paddle.

Police praise plastic peep pig in public party page.

Precious Polish pigeon paid pass for peer pudding plate.

Prepare polite pelican pile in the pail to play puddle password.

Past preschool pilgrim player put a pen in the pond to peel past pain.

Pony playmate pony pill present pencil to pull pasta.

Ponytail penguin president pump pair paste under the pillow to please the president.

Pumpkin penny pilot in pooch pajama pledge press pastry.

Plenty people pal pin pressure punch to pat people.

Pretend to punish pale patch pepper in pinch pliers pool.

Pretty poor pine puppet plow peppermint in palm path.

Perfect pop puppy with pretzel pluck pan patient.

Purple pinecone plug popcorn price to perform pane paw.

Popular plum prince in pink purse pay for pancake perfume.

Pea princess pushes pinwheel plumber panda from the period porch.

Plump pioneer panel principal had permanent peace principle to put pork pizza.

Permit possible plus puzzle print to pipe peach panic.

Post pirate person in prison pyramid pocket with peak pants.

Private postcard pit pot of permanent papa prepare peal pest.

Pitch pet poster prize poem on peanut paper.

Petal pot poet had pitcher problem to prove paperclip pear.

Point process of potato pizza had pearl piano with a parachute.

Proclaim parade with pouch poison to place in pebble pick.

Plain pickle parakeet on poke pecan perform in pound program.

Peter Piper picked a peck of pickled peppers. A peck of pickled peppers Peter Piper picked. If Peter Piper picked a peck of pickled peppers, Where's the peck of pickled peppers Peter Piper picked?

Picky people pick Peter Pan Peanut-Butter, this is the peanut-butter picky people pick.

If Pickford's packers packed a packet of crisps would the packet of crisps that Pickford's packers packed survive for two and a half years?

Pirates Private Property

Pete's pa Pete poked to the pea patch to pick a peck of peas for the poor pink pig in the pine hole pig-pen.

Supposed to be pistachio, supposed to be pistachio, supposed to be pistachio.

I'm not the fig plucker, nor the fig plucker's son, but I'll pluck figs till the fig plucker comes.

A pessimistic pest exists amidst us.

I am not a pheasant plucker, I'm a pheasant plucker's son but I'll be plucking pheasants. When the pheasant plucker's gone.

I am not the pheasant plucker, I'm the pheasant plucker's mate. I am only plucking pheasants 'cause the pheasant plucker's late.

Picky people pick Peter Pan Peanut Butter. Peter Pan Peanut is the peanut picky people pick.

Plain bun, plum bun, bun without plum.

People pledging plenty of pennies.

I'm a mother pheasant plucker, I pluck mother pheasants. I'm the most pleasant mother pheasant plucker, to ever pluck a mother pheasant. Actually, ... I'm Not the pheasant plucker, I'm the pheasant plucker's son. But I'll stay and pluck the pheasants Till the pheasant plucking 's done!

We need a plan to fan a pan; find a pan to fan, then find a fan to fan the pan, then fan the pan.

If practice makes perfect and perfect needs practice, I'm perfectly practiced and practically perfect.

How much juice does a fruit juice producer produce when a fruit juice producer produces fruit juice? We can deduce a fruit juice produces as much juice as a fruit juice produce can seduce from the fruit that produces juice.

Polly the parrot was peeling potatoes. Panda the postman popped in on his parachute. "Parcel for Polly, he said with a smile. "Papa's sent me a pair of pink pajamas!" said Polly.

A pack of pesky pixies.

If Peter Piper picked a peck of pickled peppers, how many pickled peppers did Peter Piper pick?

Is a pleasant peasant's pheasant present?

Pacific Lithograph.

Paul, please pause for proper applause.

Peggy Babcock's mummy.

People pledging plenty of pennies.

Peter poked a poker at the piper, so the piper poked pepper at Peter.

Pete's pa Pete poked to the pea patch to pick a peck of peas for the poor pink pig in the pine hole pig-pen.

Pirates Private Property

Plague-bearing prairie dogs.

Plain bun, plum bun, bun without plum.

Please pay promptly.

Plymouth sleuths thwart Luther's slithering.

Pooped purple pelicans.

Pope Sixtus VI's six texts.

Preshrunk shirts.

Preshrunk silk shirts

If Peter Piper picked a peck of pickled peppers, how many pickled peppers did Peter Piper pick? Peter poked a poker at the piper, so the piper poked pepper at Peter.

Peter Piper picked a peck of pickled pepper, a pack of pickled pepper Peter Piper picked. If Peter picked a pack of pickled pepper, where's the pack of pickled pepper Peter Piper picked?

Paul, please pause for proper applause.

A pack of pesky pixies.

Preshrunk shirts.

Peggy Babcock's mummy.

A proper cup of coffee is a proper coffee cup. A proper crop of poppies is a proper poppy-crop.

Is a pleasant peasant's pheasant present?

Pooped purple pelicans.

I'm the son of a pheasant plucker. A pheasant plucker am I. I'm only plucking pheasants. Till the pheasant plucker comes.

There's a papaya tree at the end of the port. Below the papaya tree, there's a pregnant pig. The police saw her, he blew his whistle, Pe pit Pe pit pit.

Q

Quack quitter got quick quite quill to quench queasy quarrel.

Quart quail queen quicken quilt quest to quiver quiz.

Quake queer quite quarter question to quit.

The quack quit asking quick questions.

The queen coined quick clipped quips.

The quack quit asking quick questions.

The queen coined quick clipped quips.

Quick kiss. Quicker kiss. Quickest kiss.

R

Rink with rub rod retire reason rabbit to remain ram risk-free.

Remember raccoon rode on rubber ramp received rinse retreat.

Rude return race reminds rip roll ranch for recess.

Rare remote recipe reveals ripe roller rug on the rack.

Record reverse racket rash rolling rule to remove rash race.

Rent raspberry radio recorder to review risk of ruin roof.

Reward radish red rat in a repair run room with a raft on the river.

Repeat rooster rush rhymes on refill road with a rare rattle.

Replace rag raven rib root to refuse raccoon roar.

Replay raw rail roast ripe ribbon rose in the refrigerator to relay reply.

Report rot rice ray railroad with a regular robe.

Rich razor reptile remembers Robin the raw rain reindeer.

Rotten robot rainbow research reaches Roman railway to reject rough riddle.

Read relax and respect round rock to raise reverse ride.

Real raisins with right relay rhyme rocker row.

Release rocket ring result to royal rear rake.

Reed Wade Road.

Ralph rakes leave really, really lousily.

Round brown bread, the Indian bread read "Roti". They wear "Dhoti". Round brown "Roti" is not kept in "Dhoti".

Upper roller, lower roller, upper roller, lower roller, upper roller, lower roller, ...

How many rats would the Ruskies roast if the Ruskies could roast rats? How many cats would a caddie catch if a caddie could catch cats?

Rural ruler

Rather Ruth's writhings than Roth's wrath.

Roberta ran rings around the Roman ruins.

How much pot, could a pot roast, roast if a pot roast could roast pot.

Rory the warrior and Roger the worrier were reared wrongly in a rural brewery.

Rolling red wagons

Robert Wayne Rutter

We're real rear wheels.

Real rock wall, real rock wall, real rock wall

Roy Wayne Roy Rogers Roy Rash

Truly rural, truly rural, truly rural, ...

Real weird rear wheels.

Round and round the rugged rock the ragged rascal ran.

Rattle your bottles in Rollocks' van.

Really leery, rarely Larry.

Richard's wretched ratchet wrench.

Ray Rag ran across a rough road. Across a rough road, Ray Rag ran. Where is the rough road Ray Rag ran across?

real rear wheel

The crow flew over the river with a lump of raw liver.

A real rare whale.

Ray the rat bought some red roses. He gave the roses to Rita. Rita was very happy with the lovely red roses.

A lump of red lead,

A red lead lump.

Raise Ruth's red roof.

Rattle your bottles in Rollocks' van.

Real rear wheel.

Real rock wall, real rock wall, real rock wall

Really leery, rarely Larry.

Red blood, green blood

Red Buick, blue Buick

Red lorry, yellow lorry

Rex wrecks wet rocks.

Rhys watched Ross switch his Irish wristwatch for a Swiss wristwatch.

Richard's wretched ratchet wrench.

Ripe white wheat reapers reap ripe white wheat right.

Roberta ran rings around the Roman ruins.

Roland road in a Rolls Royce.

Rolling red wagons

Rory the warrior and Roger the worrier were reared wrongly in a rural brewery.

Round and round the rugged rock the ragged rascal ran.

Round the rugged rock, the ragged rascal ran.

Rubber baby buggy bumpers.

Ruby Rugby's brother bought and brought her back some rubber baby buggy bumpers.

Rush the washing, Russel!

Ruth's red roof.

Round the rugged rocks the ragged rascals ran for rum.

Rosco the rum runner rubbed out Rudy the rat for ruining his rum-running receipts.

A lump of red lead. A red lead lump.

Round and round the rugged rocks the ragged rascal ran.

Rex wrecks wet rocks.

Rubber baby-buggy bumpers.

Raise Ruth's red roof.

Roland road in a Rolls Royce.

Rush the washing, Russel!

Ruth's red roof.

S

Sack sigh sling scorpion soldier spit scream in steer style.

Sole sad scout with slow slink sight stem subject splash.

Sign solid splatter step submarine to slip saddle scram.

Solo split slippers signal stick subway with safe scrap.

Stiff safety scrape sliver solves splash signature success.

Still scratch some silent slop sag to save such spoil.

Spoilt silk son on sudden stilt slope said scream.

Screen spoke silly slow song to suffer sting sail.

Slug screw silverware on sailboat soon stink with sponge sugar.

Sailor scribbles similar spooky sore secret to suggest stir slumber.

Simple slush scrub salad stitch spoon suit in sorrow.

Since sorry smack sports stock sale sum screws on a sailboat.

Small salmon sing at sea to sort stole spot summer.

Single smart salsa of sun horse sought to spray soap on the stomach.

Stomp smash salt seal spread soup on Sunday in the sink.

Smell sip same sour spring stone on search sunglasses.

Sprinkle stool sunflower siren smile to source siren season.

Sand spy sister stoops on the seat in smog south sunset.

Second sandal smoke sits in space square to stop sunshine.

Super-secret sandbox with smooth spaghetti squash sitter store.

Secure six snack sandwich for supper squeeze spank storm.

Story squirrel spare snag size to surely see sank the submarine.

Squirt spark snail with sap seed sizzle in stove surgery.

Sparkle stab snake with skate sat straight to see the surprise.

Stable snap sparrow strain skeleton on Saturday to seem to swallow sizzling smile.

Strange ski sauce seen to snatch stack with spat in the strange swamp.

Staff swan strap spatula to skid sneak to seize sausage.

Select straw sneakers speak with select skill on stage to save snake on Saturday.

Strawberry sniff speaker with sweat stain saw his skin himself.

Selfish sparrow in a sweater with saxophone skip seed snip to stray on the stair.

Special stream skirt snoop and say 'my stake' to sweep sell.

Sweet semi skull of scab stalk and snooze at street speck.

Spectacular tall snort skunk with swift strength scale semicircular swamp.

Stretched stamp scar swim in the sky to shallow snow with send speech.

Scare slam snowflake stand straight to sense swing speed strike.

Special staple scarecrow sent speedy snug slap to string switch.

Swollen star slash scarf snuggles to strip spell sentence.

Stripe sword scatters and stares separate spelling on a soak slate.

Spent September slave soap with symbol start to stroll scene.

Strong spice syrup with scent was served on state sled.

Starved spider struggle and sob in sleep at school service.

Social science set to spike at the station with the strange strum.

Sleigh scientist statue in sock spill stub to settle on saturated sand.

Student slice seven soda cellar with spin scissors to stay at school.

Soft spinach steal sews slick to study spider scoop on the switch.

Sick soggy spine serpent scoot slide in steam with the serious stuff.

Slim side scooter with steel stump spinner slipped in the swamp.

Silly scientist sifts stunt on steep spire sold sweet slime.

Which Swiss witch switched the Swiss wristwatches?

Silly sheep weep and sleep.

I miss my Swiss miss. My Swiss miss misses me.

Slinking, sliding, slithering slyly, Swiftly slipping through the grasses shyly, Silent but for a swish and hiss. Is the sinuous snake's leglessness.

How much squash could a sasquatch squish if a sasquatch could squish squash?

A snake sneaks to seek a snack.

Sister Susie's sewing shirts for soldiers, Such saucy soft short shirts for soldiers sister Susie sews, Some soldiers send epistles to say they'd sooner sleep on thistles, Than those saucy soft short shirts for soldiers, Sister Susie sews.

Swift shift

In shoulder surgery some surgeons sew soldiers' shoulders.

I see he sees high seas she sees.

Ice-cream: I scream, you scream, we all scream for ice cream!.

Sandwich sane witch: There's a sandwich on the sand which was sent by a sane witch.

I saw Susie: I saw Susie sitting in a shoe shine shop.

Seven slick snails: Seven slick slimy snails, slowly sliding southward.

Ah shucks, six stick shifts stuck shut!

Six thick thistle sticks.

She sells seashells on the seashore. The seashells she sells are seashore seashells.

She had shoulder surgery.

National Sheepshire Sheep Association

Which witch snitched the stitched switch for which the Swiss witch wished?

Does this shop sport short socks with spots?

Seven slick and sexy sealskin ski suits slid slowly down the slope.

Jack's nap sack strap snapped.

I saw Esau sitting on a seesaw, I saw Esau; he saw me

Sure, sir, the ship's sure shipshape, sir.

How many snacks could a snack stacker stack, if a snack stacker snacked stacked snacks?

Susie sits shinning silver shoes

The sixth sick sheik's sixth sick sheep.

Silly shoe-fly pie fans sell chilly shoe-fly pie pans.

When I went to Warsaw, I saw a saw that could outsaw any saw that I ever saw. Now, if you go to Warsaw and see a saw that could outsaw the saw I saw, I'd like to see your saw saw.

I saw a saw in Warsaw. Of all the saws I ever saw I never saw a saw that could saw, like the saw I saw in Warsaw.

Chill, Shake, Serve, ...

The sixth sick Sikh's sixth sheep is sick. The sixth sick sheik's sixth sheep 's sick. The sixth shack's sixth sick sheik's sixth sheep 's sick.

Six sticky skeletons, six sticky skeletons, six sticky skeletons, ...

Shine my city shoes!

Sniff Sesh! Sniff Sesh! Sniff Sesh!...

Silly Sally Shouldn't shave sheep she should show soon so selling sheep shaved showed she shouldn't show shaved sheep so soon.

Six slick, slim, slender saplings.

Six sick sea-serpents swam the seven seas.

Shoe section, shoe section, shoe section, ...

A smart fella, a fella smart. It takes a smart fella to say a fella smart.

She is a thistle-sifter. She has a sieve of unsifted thistles and a sieve of sifted thistles and the sieve of unsifted thistles she sifts into the sieve of sifted thistles because she is a thistle-sifter.

I slit a sheet, a sheet I slit, and on that slitted sheet, I sit.

Don't spring on the inner-spring this spring or there will be an offspring next spring.

Ed Nott was shot and Sam Shott was not. So it is better to be Shott than Nott. Some say Nott was not shot. But Shott says he shot Nott. Either the shot Shott shot at Nott was not shot, or Nott was shot. If the shot Shott shot shot Nott, Nott was shot. But if the shot Shott shot shot Shott, the shot was Shott, not Nott. However, the shot Shott shot shot not Shott - but Nott. So, Ed Nott was shot and that's hot! Is it not?

Six twin screwed steel steam cruisers.

She sells sea shells on the seashore. The seashells she sells are seashells she is sure.

From the programmer's desk: She sells C shells by the C shore.

Slick slim slippers sliding south.

The Leith police dismisseth us They thought we sought to stay; The Leith police dismisseth us They thought we'd stay all day. The Leith police dismisseth us, We both sighed sighs apiece; And the sighs that we sighed as we said goodbye were the size of the Leith police.

She sits in her slip and sips Schlitz.

I'm a sheet slitter. I slit sheets. I'm the sleekest sheet slitter that ever slit sheets.

I shot the city sheriff. I shot the city sheriff. I shot the city sheriff...

Six shining cities, six shining cities, six shining cities.

Sweet sagacious Sally Sanders said she sure saw seven segregated seaplanes sailing swiftly southward Saturday.

Swan swam over the sea. Swim, swan, swim! Swan swam back again. Well swum swan!

She slits the sheet she sits on.

A rough-coated, dough-faced, thoughtful plowman strode through the streets of Scarborough; after falling into a slough, he coughed and hiccoughed.

Knapsack strap.

Sunshine city, sunshine city, sunshine city, ...

There's a sandwich on the sand which was sent by a sane witch.

Sister Suzie sewing shirts for soldiers. Such skill as sewing shirts. Our shy young sister Suzie shows. Some soldiers send epistles. Say they'd rather sleep in thistles. Than the saucy, soft short shirts for soldiers Sister Suzie sews.

The soldier's shoulder surely hurts!

She sees seas slapping shores.

Mr. See owned a saw and Mr. Soar owned a seesaw. Now See's saw sawed Soar's seesaw before Soar saw See.

Singing Sammy sung songs on sinking sand.

Scissors sizzle, thistles sizzle.

How many sheets could a sheet slitter slit if a sheet slitter could slit sheets?

Sounding by sound is a sound method of sounding sounds.

This is the sixth zebra snoozing thoroughly.

Salty broccoli, salty broccoli, salty broccoli ....

I saw Esau kissing Kate. I saw Esau, he saw me, and she saw I saw Esau.

A slimy snake slithered down the sandy Sahara.

Suzie Seaworld's fish-sauce shop sells unsifted thistles for thistle-sifters to sift.

She said she should sit.

I see a sea down by the seashore. But which sea do you see down by the seashore?

She sees cheese.

Seven sleazy shysters in sharkskin suits sold sheared sealskins to seasick sailors.

Silly sheep weep and sleep.

The seething sea ceaseth; thus the seething sea sufficeth us.

I slit a sheet, a sheet I slit, upon a slitted sheet I sit.

I'm a sock cutter and I cut socks. I'm a sock cutter and I cut socks. I'm a sock cutter and I cut socks.

How may saws could a see-saw saw if a see-saw could saw saws?

Shut up the shutters and sit in the shop.

But she as far surpasseth Sycorax, As great'st does least.

Seth at Sainsbury's sells thick socks.

Six sick hicks nick six slick bricks with picks and sticks.

Stupid superstition!

If Stu chews shoes, should Stu choose the shoes he chews?

Seventy seven benevolent elephants

I scream, you scream, we all scream for ice-cream!

Six sleek swans swam swiftly southwards

She saw Sherif's shoes on the sofa. But was she so sure she saw Sherif's shoes on the sofa?

Three short sword sheaths.

I stood sadly on the silver steps of Burgess's fish sauce shop, mimicking him hiccuping, and wildly welcoming him within.

As I was in Arkansas I saw a saw that could out saw any saw I ever saw saw. If you happen to be in Arkansas and see a saw that can out saw the saw I saw saw I'd like to see the saw you saw saw.

Seven slick slimy snakes slowly sliding southward.

Six sticky sucker sticks.

I saw Susie sitting in a shoe shine shop. Where she sits she shines, and where she shines she sits.

Sam is sad today. Sam has lost his star. Sam is sad without his star. So Sam's dad gave him a new star. Sam is happy now.

"Go my son, and shut the shutter."

"I cannot shut it any shutter."

"The shutter's shut," the son did utter,

A woman to her son did utter,

No shark shares swordfish steak.

No shipshape ships shop stocks shop-soiled shirts.

Sally sells seashells by the seashore.

Sam's shop stocks short spotted socks.

Sarah saw a shot-silk sash shop full of shot-silk sashes

Scissors sizzle, thistles sizzle.

Seized his knees and sneezed.

Selfish sharks sell shut shellfish.

Selfish shellfish.

Seth at Sainsbury's sells thick socks.

Seth's sharp spacesuit shrank.

Seven Silly Swans Swam Silently Seaward

Seven sleazy shysters in sharkskin suits sold sheared sealskins to seasick sailors.

Seven slick slimy snakes slowly sliding southward.

Seventy-seven benevolent elephants

Sexist sixties.

She ceased shining shoes and socks, for shoes and socks shock Susan.

She had shoulder surgery.

She said she should sit!

She saw Sherif's shoes on the sofa. But was she so sure she saw Sherif's shoes on the sofa?

She sees cheese.

She sees seas slapping shores.

She sells sea shells by the seashore.

She sells seashells on the seashore. The seashells she sells are seashore seashells.

She sells Swiss sweets.

She sifted thistles through her thistle-sifter.

She sits in her slip and sips Schlitz.

She slits the sheet she sits on.

She stood on the balcony inexplicably mimicking him hiccuping, and amicably welcoming him home.

Sheena leads, Sheila needs.

Shelter for six sick scenic sightseers.

Sherman shops at cheap chop suey shops.

Shoe section, shoe section, shoe section, ...

Shredded Swiss cheese.

Shut up the shutters and sit in the shop.

Shy Shelly says she shall sew sheets.

Silly sheep weep and sleep.

Sinful Caesar sipped his snifter,

Singing Sammy sung songs on sinking sand.

Sister Susie sewing shirts for soldiers.

Six crisp snacks.

Six quick sneezes, six quick sneezes, six quick sneezes

Six sharp smart sharks.

Six shimmering sharks sharply striking shins.

Six shining cities, six shining cities, six shining cities.

Six short slow shepherds.

Six shy shavers sheared six shy sheep.

Six sick hicks nick six slick bricks with picks and sticks.

Six sick sea-serpents swam the seven seas.

Six sick sheep.

Six sick slick slim sycamore saplings.

Six sleek swans swam swiftly southwards

Six slimy snails sailed silently.

Six slippery snails, slid slowly seaward.

Six sticky sucker sticks.

Six thick thistle sticks.

Six twin screwed steel steam cruisers.

Sixish.

Sly Sam slurps Sally's soup.

Spark plug car park.

Stagecoach stops.

Strange strategic statistics.

Such a shapeless sash!

Sunshine city, sunshine city, sunshine city, ...

Sure the ship's shipshape, sir.

Susan shineth shoes and socks; socks and shoes shines Susan.

Suzie Seaworld's fish-sauce shop sells unsifted thistles for thistle-sifters to sift.

Swatch watch

Sweet sagacious Sally Sanders said she sure saw seven segregated seaplanes sailing swiftly southward Saturday.

Switch watch, wristwatch.

Synonym cinnamon.

The sixth sheik's sixth sheep's sick.

Should saucy sharks seek shelter soon?

The sixth sick sheik's sixth sheep's sick.

She sits and shines shoes. And when she sits she shines all day

A skunk sat on a stump. The skunk thought the stump stunk. The stump thought the skunk stunk.

Sister Suzy's sewing shirts for soldiers. Such skill at sewing shirts my shy young sister Suzy shows. Some soldiers send epistles. Saying they'd sooner sleep on thistles. Than the short serge shirts for soldiers shy young sister Suzy sews.

Sister Susie went to sea. To see the sea, you see. The sea she saw was a saucy sea. A sort of saucy sea saw she.

Give me the gift of a grip-top sock, A clip drape shipshape tip-top sock. Not your spin slick slapstick slipshod stock, But a plastic, elastic grip-top sock. None of your fantastic slack swap slop, From a slapdash flash cash haberdash shop. Not a knick-knack knitlock knockkneed knickerbocker sock, With a mock-shot blob-mottled trick-ticker top clock. Not a super sweet seersucker rucksack sock, Not a spot-speckled frog-freckled cheap sheik's sock, Off a hodgepodge moss-blotched scotch-botched block. Nothing slipshod drip drop flip flop or glip glop, Tip me to a tip-top grip top sock.

Mr. See owned a saw, And Mr. Soar owned a seesaw. Now See's saw sawed Soar's seesaw before Soar saw See, which made Soar sore. Had Soar seen See's saw before See sawed Soar's seesaw, See's saw would not have sawed Soar's seesaw.

She was a thistle sifter and sifted thistles through a thistle sieve.

Shy Shelly says she shall sew sheets.

These sheep shouldn't sleep in a shack; Sheep should sleep in a shed.

The sinking steamer sank.

Six sharp smart sharks.

Six shimmering sharks sharply striking shins.

Six short slow shepherds.

Six slippery snails slid slowly seaward.

Six sticky sucker sticks.

Six twin-screwed steel steam cruisers.

Sly Sam slurps Sally's soup.

Sherman shops at cheap chop suey shops.

Selfish sharks sell shut shellfish.

Seth's sharp spacesuit shrank.

Sexist sixties.

She sells Swiss sweets.

She sells sea shells by the seashore.

Sally sells seashells by the seashore.

Six crisp snacks.

Stagecoach stops.

Strange strategic statistics.

No shipshape ships shop stocks shop-soiled shirts.

No shark shares swordfish steak.

Short folder.

Sister Susie sewing shirts for soldiers.

Six sick sheep.

Six shy shavers sheared six shy sheep.

The sixth sheik's sixth sheep's sick.

A woman to her son did utter, "Go my son, and shut the shutter." "The shutter's shut," the son did utter, "I cannot shut it any shutter."

Spark plug car park.

Such a shapeless sash!

Sinful Caesar sipped his snifter, seized his knees and sneezed.

A skunk sat on a stump. The stump thunk the skunk stunk. The skunk thunk the stump stunk.

Sheila is selling her shop at the seashore. For shops at the seashore are so sure to lose. Now she's not so sure of what she should be selling! Should Sheila sell seashells or should she sell shoes?

If he slipped, should she slip?

Miss Smith dismisseth us.

I'm a sheet slitter. I slit sheets. I am the best sheet slitter that ever slit a sheet. I slit the sheet, the sheet I slit. Upon the slitted sheet I sit.

The swan swam over the sea. Swim swan swim. Swan swam back again. Well swum, swan.

Synonym cinnamon.

Six thick thistle sticks.

Mr. See and Mr. Soar were old friends. See a saw and Soar owned a seesaw. Now See's saw sawed Soar's seesaw before Soar saw See, which made Soar sore. Had Soar seen See's saw before See saw Soar's seesaw, then See's saw would not have sawed Soar's seesaw. But See saw Soar's seesaw before Soar saw See's saw so See's saw sawed Soar's seesaw. It was a shame to let See see. Soar so sore because See's saw sawed Soar's seesaw.

SH

Shameful shell shirt shopkeeper had seen shovel sleeves and shawl to sense shudder.

She shows silk shiver in the shelter on sun shore to shuffle shampoo soup in shade.

Short shocked shamrock shepherd shower in the sea with shushing sheaf under the shadow.

Shady shocking sheriff with shear shape had shown soon shorten shut salsa.

Shoe showroom in shield shed shag shown sheen shortly after shutdown.

Shaggy sore shark with shoelace shred short sick sheep in shutter sink.

Sorry sharp shoemaker shot simple sheepdog to shut sharp shin slowly.

Sheepish sentry with shaky shoestring should shrink sharp sari spray.

Shiny seer shoulder shall shrink sample but surely shatter small shook solution.

Shallow shingle shave sheet with soup shouldn't have shone six shrivel.

Shaver shipshape shoot shout ski shrub on the shelf to save shamble skeleton.

After shove shaving, she'll shop shovel in selected shambles to shrug seer.

Santa's Short Suit Shrunk.

Dr. Johnson and Mr. Johnson, after great consideration, came to the conclusion that the Indian nation beyond the Indian Ocean is back in education because the chief occupation is cultivation.

Whoever slit the sheets is a good sheet slitter.

Preshrunk silk shirts.

There once was a man who had a sister, his name was Mr. Fister. Mr. Fister's sister sold seashells by the seashore. Mr. Fister didn't sell sea shells, he sold silk sheets. Mr. Fister told his sister that he sold six silk sheets to six shieks. The sister of Mr. Fister said I sold six shells to six shieks too!

Sally sells seashells by the seashore. But if Sally sells sea shells by the sea shore then where are the seashells Sally sells?

She stood on the steps of Burgess's Fish Sauce Shop, mimicking him hiccuping and amicably welcoming him in.

Sally is a sheet slitter, she slits sheets.

She sells sea shells on the sea shore; The shells that she sells are sea shells I'm sure. So if she sells sea shells on the seashore, I'm sure that the shells are seashore shells.

Sheila is selling her shop at the seashore. For shops at the seashore are so sure to lose And she's not so sure of what she should be selling Should Sheila sell seashells or should she sell shoes

Squash the fish and mash it well. Crush, smash, what a smell! Spice the fish and make a wish. Swish it round in the dish. Push the button, let it cook. Rush, rush to have a wash.

Suzie, Suzie, working in a shoeshine shop. All day long she sits and shines, all day long she shines and sits, and sits and shines, and shines and sits, and sits and shines, and shines and sits. Suzie, Suzie, working in a shoeshine shop.

T

Triple tower tape with tunnel tights had total temper told teller tab to take tinder.

Triplet toy turkey with tomato tar took tile temperature on the table in town.

Tardy tilt tomboy to turn troll with a tablet in the temple.

Trace timber target tempts tack tomorrow for troop turning.

Ten-time tone trot moves turnip tart tackle on track.

Turtle with trouble tongue tend to task tack with a timer on the tractor.

Tender trout with tusk tact trade timid taste tonight.

Tad truck in traffic with tin tattoo tweet about tennis too.

Tinsel tadpole took the tense trail to true tax twig.

Tiny twin taxi on trumpet train in tent ate taffy.

Tenth trap trunk tip twine with tea tag to toot.

Trust twinkle tepee tooth with the tail to teach trash thrust.

Top travels tire twirl to take teacher's terrible truth.

Terrific teacup tray tries to twist the tale of tissue topic.

Teapot title treasures the test two for tub-torch talent.

Tube tornado tends to tear the textbook to talk about the treat.

Tall toad in tug tick toss to tease tenth timid tree.

Teddy had a ticket for total toast in triangular tugboat tamale.

Today it is tough to tickle and tame teen tulip tribe.

Teeth to toe trick tide to tour tumble tan.

Tangerine telephone with tow tie trim tummy together.

Tangle trinket taken to toilet towards tiger in television trimming tuna.

Token tight tap towel told to tune the trip or tell tadpole.

Tie twine to three tree twigs.

I thought the haughty Professor Tortoise taught ontology, but the naughty Tortoise taught us tautology.

I have got a date: I have got a date at a quarter to eight; I'll see you at the gate, so don't be late.

Kanta is a Masai girl. She can tie a tie and untie a tie. If Kanta can tie a tie and untie a tie, why can't I tie a tie and untie a tie?

Fred Threlfall's thirty-five fine threads are finer threads than Fred Threlfall's thirty- five thick threads.

Thirty-six thick silk threads

Kantai can tie a tie. If Kantai can tie a tie, why can't I tie a tie like Kantai can tie a tie.

The two-toed tree toad tried to tread where the three-toed tree toad trod.

Tricky Tristan tracked a trail of tiny turtles. How many tiny turtles did Tricky Tristan track? Tricky Tristan tracked twenty-two tiny turtles; that's how many tiny turtles tricky Tristan tracked.

Thirty-three thousand feathers on a thrushes throat.

Thomas Tattamus took two T's to tie two tots to two tall trees.

Never trust a sloppy crust, a squally gust, ships that rust, or birds with lust. But if you must, you may trust to go bust, and back to dust, which serves you just.

Mister Twister's tongue twisters, ...

Theodore Thistle threw three thorny thistles. How many thorny thistles did Theodore Thistle throw?

Tell a tall tale of a tall tailed dog, that told Tim it tap a tall ale and thump the top of Tim's tomb.

They think that their teeth get thinner at times they want to taste thick meat.

How many tow trucks could a tow truck tow if a tow truck could tow tow trucks.

She thrust three thousand thistles through the thick of her thumb.

Tie a knot, tie a knot. Tie a tight, tight knot. Tie a knot in the shape of naught.

There are two minutes difference from four to two to two to two, from two to two to two, too.

A twister of twists once twisted a twist, and the twist that he twisted was a three-twisted twist. now in twisting this twist, if a twist should untwist, would the twist that untwisted untwist the twists?

Twelve twins twirled twelve twigs.

Announcement at Victoria Station, London: "Two to two to Tooting too!"

Don't trouble trouble, until trouble troubles you! If you trouble trouble, triple trouble troubles you!

Theophilus Thadeus Thistledown, the successful thistle-sifter, while sifting a sieve- full of unsifted thistles, thrust three thousand thistles through the thick of his thumb. Now, if Theophilus Thadeus Thistledown, the successful thistle-

sifter, thrust three thousand thistles through the thick of his thumb, see that thou, while sifting a sieve- full of unsifted thistles, thrust not three thousand thistles through the thick of thy thumb.

King Thistle stuck a thousand thistles in the thistle of his thumb. A thousand thistles King Thistle stuck in the thistle of his thumb. If King Thistle stuck a thousand thistles in the thistle of his thumb, How many thistles did King Thistle stick in the thistle of his thumb?

A Tudor who tooted the flute tried to tutor two tooters to toot. Said the two to the tutor, "Is it harder to toot or to tutor two tooters to toot?"

Mrs. Puggy Wuggy has a square cut punt. Not a punt cut square, Just a square cut punt. It's round in the stern and blunt in the front. Mrs. Puggy Wuggy has a square cut punt.

Tim, the thin twin tinsmith.

Thin sticks, thick bricks

I thought a thought. But the thought I thought. Wasn't the thought I thought I thought. If the thought I thought I thought, Had been the thought I thought, I wouldn't have thought I thought.

To begin to toboggan, first buy a toboggan. But don't buy too big a toboggan. Too big a toboggan is too big a toboggan to buy to begin to toboggan.

Three Tree Turtles. Three tree turtles took turns talking tongue twisters. If three tree turtles took turns talking

tongue twisters, where have the twisters the three tree turtles talked?

Tommy, Tommy, toiling in a tailor's shop.

All day long he fits and tucks, all day long he tucks and fits,

and fits and tucks, and tucks and fits, and fits and tucks, and tucks and fits. Tommy, Tommy, toiling in a tailor's shop.

Terry Teeter, a teeter-totter teacher, taught her daughter Tara to teeter-totter, but Tara Teeter didn't teeter-totter as Terry Teeter taught her to.

What a terrible tongue twister, what a terrible tongue twister, what a terrible tongue twister...

Elizabeth's birthday is on the third Thursday of this month.

Mr. Tongue Twister tried to train his tongue to twist and turn, and twit a twat, to learn the letter "T".

Two tried and true tridents

Thirty-three thirsty, thundering thoroughbreds thumped Mr. Thurber on Thursday.

Tie twine to three tree twigs.

Caution: Wide Right Turns seen on semi-tractor trailers.

I thought, I thought of thinking of thanking you.

He threw three balls.

Tom threw Tim three thumbtacks.

He threw three free throws.

Two tiny tigers take two taxis to town.

Tommy Tucker tried to tie Tammy's Turtles tie.

Old Mr. Hunt had a cuddy punt Not a cuddy punt but a hunt punt cuddy.

Thin grippy thick slippery.

A tree toad loved a she-toad, Who lived up in a tree. He was a three-toed tree toad, But a two-toed toad was she. The three-toed tree toad tried to win, The two-toed she-toad's heart, For the three-toed tree toad loved the ground, That the two-toed tree toad trod. But the three-toed tree toad tried in vain. He couldn't please her whim. From her tree toad bower, With her two-toed power, The she-toad vetoed him.

There those thousand thinkers were thinking where did those other three thieves go through.

Two to two to Toulouse?

Thirty-three thousand people think that Thursday is their thirtieth birthday.

If Kantie can tie a tie and untie a tie, why can't I tie a tie and untie a tie as Katie can.

Tommy, Tommy, toiling in a tailor's shop. All day long he fits and tucks, all day long he tucks and fits, and fits and tucks, and tucks and fits, and fits and tucks, and tucks and fits. Tommy, Tommy, toiling in a tailor's shop.

Tim the tiger talks on the phone. His friend is Tom the turtle. Tom and Tim have tea. After tea, they play with bat and ball.

Do thick tinkers think?

I shot three shy thrushes.

Tacky tractor-trailer trucks.

Ten tame tadpoles tucked tightly together in a thin tall tin.

Thank the other three brothers of their father's mother's brother's side.

that is the way you spell New York.

The batter with the butter is the batter that is better!

The big bad baby brought the bought black blanket back

The bootblack bought the black boot back.

The crow flew over the river with a lump of raw liver.

The epitome of femininity.

The Leith police dismisseth us.

The myth of Miss Muffet.

The ochre ogre ogled the poker.

The queen in green screamed.

The ruddy widow really wants ripe watermelon and red roses when winter arrives.

The sawingest saw I ever saw saw.

The sea ceaseth, but it sufficeth us.

The seething sea ceaseth; thus the seething sea sufficeth us.

The seething seas ceaseth and twiceth the seething seas sufficeth us.

The sixth sick sheik's sixth sheep's sick.

The soldier's shoulder surely hurts!

The soldiers shouldered shooters on their shoulders.

The thirty-three thieves thought that they thrilled the throne throughout Thursday.

The two-twenty-two train tore through the tunnel.

Thelma sings the theme song.

There goes one tough top cop!

There those thousand thinkers were thinking where did those other three thieves go through.

There those thousand thinkers were thinking how did the other three thieves go through.

There was a little witch which switched from Chichester to Ipswich.

There was a minimum of cinnamon in the aluminum pan.

There's a sandwich on the sand which was sent by a sane witch.

These thousand tricky tongue twisters trip thrillingly off the tongue

They both, though, have thirty-three thick thimbles to thaw.

They have left the thrift shop, and lost both their theatre tickets and the volume of valuable licenses and coupons for free theatrical frills and thrills.

Thieves seize skis.

Thin sticks, thick bricks

Thirty-three thirsty, thundering thoroughbreds thumped Mr. Thurber.

This is a zither.

This is the sixth zebra snoozing thoroughly.

Three free throws.

Three short sword sheaths.

Three twigs twined tightly.

Tie twine to three tree twigs.

Tim, the thin twin tinsmith

Tim, the thin twin tinsmith.

To have a truck to truck two trucks of the truck.

Tom threw Tim three thumbtacks.

Tommy Tucker tried to tie Tammy's Turtles tie.

Tommy, Tommy, toiling in a tailor's shop.

Tragedy strategy.

Truly rural.

Twelve standard stainless steel twin screw cruisers.

Twelve twins twirled twelve twigs.

Twice we tripped toys.

Two tiny tigers take two taxis to town.

Two to two to Toulouse?

Two toads, totally tired.

Two tried and true tridents

Two Truckee truckers truculently truckling

Theophilus Thistle, the successful thistle sifter, successfully sifted some thistles.

Thistle sticks sixty-six thousand and six thistle sticks. Theophulous Thistle, the thistle sifter thrust a thousand thistles through the thick of his thumb.

What a to-do to die today, at a minute or two to two; A thing distinctly hard to say, but harder still to do. For they'll beat a tattoo, at twenty to two. A rat-tat-tat- tat-tat-tat- tat-tat tattoo. And a dragon will come when he hears the drum, at a minute or two to two today, at a minute or two to two.

The lips, the teeth, the tip of the tongue, the tip of the tongue, the teeth, the lips.

Thieves seize skis.

Three free throws. Three gray geese in the green grass grazing. Grays were the geese and green was the grass. Three twigs twined tightly. Tim, the thin twin tinsmith.

Toy boat. Toy boat. Toy boat.

I shot three shy thrushes.

There goes one tough top cop!

Do thick tinkers think?

Ten tame tadpoles tucked tightly together in a thin tall tin.

From a plate of wheat, three sad tigers ate wheat.

Theopholus Thistle, the successful thistle sifter, successfully sifted some thistles.

Truly rural.

Three free throws.

Thelma sings the theme song.

Toy boat.

Tacky tractor-trailer trucks.

Twice we tripped toys.

A tutor who tooted the flute. Tried to tutor two tooters to toot. Said the two to the tutor, "Is it harder to toot, or to tutor two tooters to toot?"

Twelve standard stainless steel twin screw cruisers.

TH

Thank thigh thermometer throwing terrific thought threat with a thumb on the tight throne.

Three thousand thimble throw thunder typhoon to thaw thick tornado.

Thin tall theater thief threw thorn in the towel on the throat with thread.

The thirty-three thieves thought that they thrilled the throne throughout Thursday.

Something in a thirty-acre thermal thicket of thorns and thistles thumped and thundered threatening the three-D thoughts of Matthew the thug - although, theatrically, it was only the thirteen-thousand thistles and thorns through the underneath of his thigh that the thirty-year-old thug thought of that morning.

There those thousand thinkers were thinking how did the other three thieves go through.

Dear mother, give your other udder to my other brother.

Three tired tigers try to throw three trees.

Thrifty Theophilus, the theocratic thistle sifter, thrice thrust three thousand thistles through the slick thick of his softly throbbing thumb.

The third time the three three-toed tree toads tried tying their toes together, the third three-toed tree toad tied the two three-toed trees toads toes to the third toad's toes. Then the two tied three-toed tree toads told the third three-toed tree toad that tying their toes together thrilled them to their toe tips.

I thought of thinking: I thought, I thought of thinking of thanking you.

Thirty-three thieves: The thirty-three thieves thought that they thrilled the throne throughout Thursday.

Thelma woke up on Thursday night and said, "I think I heard a thump. It must be a thief. I told Theo a thousand times to lock the window." She took a stick and pushed open the door with her thumb.

My dame hath a lame tame crane. My dame hath a crane that is lame. Oh gentle Jane, doth my dame's lame tame crane leave and come home again?

The teacher thought and thought and thought And nobody knew the thought he thought. 33 333- Thirty- three thousand three hundred and thirty- three.

V

Vacant vegetable volume vent tries to vet the value of vitamin vine.

Vacation vehicle violet van is a vocabulary verb for video vote.

Veil vanilla violin voice vow verse in vacuum to view very violent West.

Vein vision valentine vanishes in vowel volcano at the beaten baboon.

Velvet vase balloon valley visits volleyball villain in the vineyard to vest vocal control.

Very rare vagrant wader.

Velvet Revolver Velvet Revolver Velvet Revolver...

An illusory vision is a visionary illusion. Is it?

The van is violet. It's a violet van. The violet van will take us to the vet. The vet will see out the violet van. He will say 'what a lovely violet van!'

Valuable valley villas.

What veteran ventriloquist whistles.

Very well, very well, very well ...

Vincent vowed vengeance very vehemently.

Vinny the vet was drinking some water. The water fell on the van. Vinny the vet took a white cloth and wiped the wet spot.

W

Weed watermelon wants to wade in the water to wiggle wisdom worm.

Wild wave waffle war was welcome where wise worms were weak.

Warm wax wag wild in a weekend which will wish to worry less.

Willow wagon warns worst weep while wishing winter wit on the way.

We weigh witch waist weight with worth warning to whine and wilt.

Wounded weak warrior welcome win but wait to whip worst bone with banana.

Wizard waiter with whirl wart try to wind wealth well within wax limits.

Wear wolf went to wake and would whisper Wishlist to the widow in the window.

Windy women wash and whistle wax weapon to walk the windpipe of the wealthy palace window.

White wind wall wonders the weakness of weather to washcloth with the wing.

Wooden wink whale weave waste of wallet to wonder why.

World wide web wonder what word to watch white walnut at Walter city.

Weighty walrus wife in water wipe wedding wheat work to wink in wit.

On Wednesday, Vendy's white wife in wheel wig started to win the world with a wand in wire waterfall.

Who washed Washington's white woolen underwear when Washington's washerwoman went west?

Esau Wood saw a wood saw, saw wood, as no wood saw would saw wood. If Esau Wood saw a wood saw, saw wood, as no wood saw would saw wood, where is the wood saw which would saw wood, as no wood saw would saw wood.

There was a writer called Wright, he taught his son to write Wright right: "It's not right to write Wright 'Rite', please try to write Wright right!"

A wooden worm wouldn't be worthy of worship but would he if he wondered and worried about what he would be worthy of if he wasn't wooden?

Washington's washwoman washed Washington's wash while Washington's wife went west.

Which Witch snitched the Snitch Witch? Or did the Snitch Witch snitch the Witch? If the Snitch Witch snitched the Witch. Then which Witch did the Snitch Witch snitch?

Free Ritz wristwatch.

I wish to wish the wish you wish to wish, but if you wish the wish the witch wishes, I won't wish the wish you wish to wish.

Willy's wooden whistle wouldn't whistle when Willy went wild.

Wilson Winston winced whilst he minced a squinting prince.

Two witches, two watches: If two witches would watch two watches, which witch would watch which watch?

Whether the weather: Whether the weather be fine, or whether the weather be not. Whether the weather be cold, or whether the weather be hot. We'll weather the weather whether we like it or not.

Nature watcher: Out in the pasture the nature watcher watches the catcher. While the catcher watches the pitcher, who pitches the balls. Whether the temperature's up or whether the temperature's down, the nature watcher, the catcher and the pitcher are always around. The pitcher pitches, the catcher catches and the watcher watches. So, whether the temperature's rises or whether the temperature falls the nature watcher just watches the catcher w ho's watching the pitcher who's watching the balls.

Wish to wish: I wish to wish the wish you wish to wish, but if you wish the wish the witch wishes, I won't wish the wish you wish to wish.

Which wristwatches are Swiss wristwatches?

While we were walking, we were watching window washers wash Washington's windows with warm washing water.

Ripe white wheat reapers reap ripe white wheat right.

Whether the weather be fine or whether the weather be not. Whether the weather be cold or whether the weather be hot. We'll weather the weather whether we like it or not.

If two witches would watch two watches, which witch would watch which watch?

A loyal warrior will rarely worry about why we rule.

There was a little witch which switched from Chichester to Ipswich.

Esau Wood sawed wood. All the wood Esau Wood saw, Esau Wood would saw. All the wood Wood saw, Esau sought to saw. One day Esau Wood's wood-saw would saw no wood. So, Esau Wood sought a new wood-saw. The new wood-saw would saw wood. Oh, the wood Esau Wood would saw. Esau sought a saw that would saw wood as no other wood-saw would saw. And Esau found a saw that would saw as no other wood-saw would saw. And Esau Wood sawed wood.

A skunk sat on a stump and thunk the stump stunk, but the stump thunk the skunk stunk.

Sweater weather, leather weather.

We will learn why her lowly lone, worn yarn loom will rarely earn immoral money.

How much wood would a woodchuck chuck if a woodchuck would chuck wood? A woodchuck would chuck how much a woodchuck would chuck if a woodchuck would chuck wood.

Switch watch, wristwatch.

I wish I were what I was when I wished I were what I am.

Irish wristwatch.

Which witch whined when the wine was spilled on the wailing whale?

"I don't care a whit for your wit or whims," said Warren Wharton.

Whether the weather be cold. Or whether the weather be hot. Whatever the weather we'll weather the weather. Whether we like it or not.

William always wears a very warm woolen vest in winter.

Victor, however, will never wear woolen underwear, even in the Wild West.

Which witch wished which wish?

If two witches were watching two watches, which witch would watch which watch?

I wish to wish the wish you wish to wish, but if you wish the wish the witch wishes, I won't wish the wish you wish to wish.

World Wide Web

Wayne went to Wales to watch walruses.

Willy's real rear wheel

Why do you cry, Willy? Why do you cry? Why, Willy? Why, Willy? Why, Willy? Why?

Very well, very well, very well ...

Rhys watched Ross switch his Irish wristwatch for a Swiss wristwatch.

I wish to wash my Irish wristwatch.

Gig whip, gig whip, gig whip, ...

Wow, race winners really want red wine right away!

The ruddy widow really wants ripe watermelon and red roses when winter arrives.

Willie's really weary.

Will you, William? Will you, William? Will you, William? Can't you, don't you, won't you, William?

I wish you were a fish in my dish.

We won, we won, we won, we won, ...

How much myrtle would a wood turtle hurdle if a wood turtle could hurdle myrtle? A wood turtle would hurdle as much myrtle as a wood turtle could hurdle if a wood turtle could hurdle myrtle.

Which wristwatch is a Swiss wristwatch?

Should Jim Wright decide to write right rite, then Wright would write right rite, which Wright has the right to copyright. Duplicating that rite would copy Wright right rite, and violate copyright, which Wright would have the right to right.

Wanda the whale swims all day in the ocean. Wanda likes to live in water. Wanda likes to eat Willy the fish. Willy always runs away from Wanda.

Real wristwatch straps.

Wally Winkle wriggles his white, wrinkled wig.

Was the saw I saw saw in Arkansas.

Wash Washington's windows with warm washing water.

Wayne went to Wales to watch walruses.

We surely shall see the sunshine soon.

Well they can't carry berries

We're real rear wheels.

Wetter weather never weathered wetter weather better.

What a shame such a shapely sash should such shabby stitches show.

What time does the wristwatch strap shop shut?

When Washington's washerwoman went west?

When you write copy you have the right to copyright the copy you write. ...

Which rich wicked witch wished the wicked wish?

Which witch watched which watch?

Which witch wished which wicked wish?

Which wristwatch is a Swiss wristwatch?

While we were walking, we were watching window washers

While we were walking, we were watching window washers wash Washington's windows with warm washing water.

Who washed Washington's white woolen underwear

Whoever slit the sheets is a good sheet slitter.

Why can't I tie a tie and untie a tie as Katie can.

Will you, William?

Willie's really weary.

Wow, race winners really want red wine right away!

"Will you walk a little faster," said the whiting to the snail. "There's a porpoise close behind us and he's treading on my tail. See how eagerly the lobsters and the turtles all advance.

They are waiting on a shingle; will you come and join the dance? Will you, won't you, will you, won't you. Will you join the dance? won't you, will you, you Won't, you will. Won't you join the dance?"

Which witch wished which wicked wish? Which wristwatches are Swiss wristwatches? While we were walking, we were watching window washers wash Washington's windows with warm washing water. Whistle for the thistle sifter. White eraser? Right away, sir!

Which rich wicked witch wished the wicked wish? Which wristwatch is a Swiss wristwatch? Which witch watched which watch? Irish wrist-watch. Real wristwatch straps. If two witches were watching two watches, which witch would watch which watch?

Wetter weather never weathered wetter weather better. Wally Winkle wriggles his white, wrinkled wig. How much wood would a woodchuck chuck, if a woodchuck could chuck wood?

X

The ex-egg examiner.

X-Mas wrecks perplex and vex.

X-ray checks clear chests.

Ex-disk jockey.

Y

This year, you say yes, yip or yo-yo to yak yelling in the yard.

Your yum yarn yogurt is yet to yell at yam.

Yellow yolk yield yank to yawn in youth.

How many yaks could a yak pack, pack if a yak pack could pack yaks?

Spell New York: Knife and a fork, bottle and a cork, that is the way you spell New York.

Understand: If you understand, say "understand". If you don't understand, say "don't understand". But if you understand and say "don't understand". How do I understand that you understand?

Did you see a yellow yacht? It belongs to Yuri the Yak. Yuri the Yak loves yolk and yam with tea.

Local yokel jokes.

Yanking yellow yo-yos.

Yellow leather, yellow feather, yellow lemon.

Z

Zany the zebra zap zig-zag in the zoo.

Zero zeal of zoom zip the zone.

This is a zither.

Fuzzy Wuzzy was a bear, Fuzzy Wuzzy had no hair, Fuzzy Wuzzy wasn't very fuzzy, was he?

Zithers slither slowly south.

Zizzi's zippy zipper zips.

This is a zither. Is this a zither?

Vowels and Mixed Phrases

The first set of tongue twisters would contain phrases starting with vowels i.e. a, e, i, o, u and mixed phrases

A

Sam the fat cat with a hat. He can see the jam. The jam is in a pan. The pan is on a mat. Sam the fat cat likes to jam. Sam sat on the mat and had the jam.

"What ails Alex?" asks Alice.

A big black bear sat on a big black bug.

A big black bug bit a big black bear and made the big black bear bleed blood.

A big black bug bit a big black bear and the big black bear bled blood

A big black bug bit a big black bear, made the big black bear bleed blood.

A black bloke's back brake-block broke.

A bloke's back bike brake block broke.

A bloke's bike back brake block broke.

A box of biscuits, a batch of mixed biscuits

A lump of red leather, a red leather lump

A lusty lady loved a lawyer and longed to lure him from his laboratory.

A noise annoys an oyster, but a noisy noise annoys an oyster more!

A noisy noise annoys an oyster.

A nurse anesthetist unearthed a nest.

A pessimistic pest exists amidst us.

A pleasant place to place a place is a place where a place is pleased to be placed.

A proper cup of coffee from a proper copper coffee pot.

A real rare whale.

A skunk sat on a stump and thunk the stump stunk, but the stump thunk the skunk stunk.

A slimy snake slithered down the sandy Sahara.

A turbot's not a burbot, for a turbot's a butt, but a burbot's not.

Ah shucks, six stick shifts stuck shut!

Alice asks for axes.

An elephant was asphyxiated in the asphalt.

Ann and Andy's anniversary is in April.

Are our oars oak?

Argyle Gargoyle

As one black bug, bled blue, black blood. The other black bug bled blue.

As the sunshine shone on the side of the shot-silk sash shop.

If I assist a sister-assistant, will the sister's sister-assistant assist me?

Around the rugged rocks the ragged rascal ran.

If I assist a sister-assistant, will the sister's sister-assistant assist me?

"What ails Alex?" asks Alice. Alice asks for axes.

Arnold Palmer, Arnold Palmer, Arnold Palmer, ...

Ann and Andy's anniversary is in April.

E

Ken had a hen and Jen had a hen. Len had a hen but Ben had ten hens! When Ken and Jen and Len met Ben, how many hens did they all have then?

Each Easter Eddie eats eighty Easter eggs.

Ed had edited it.

Eddie edited it.

Eleven benevolent elephants

Elizabeth has eleven elves in her elm tree.

Elizabeth's birthday is on the third Thursday of this month.

Ere her ear hears her err, here ears err here.

Excited executioner exercising his excising powers excessively.

Esau Wood would saw Wood. Oh, the wood that Wood would saw! One day Esau Wood saw a saw saw wood as no other wood-saw Wood ever saw would saw wood. Of all the wood-saws. Wood ever saw saw wood, Wood never saw a wood-saw that would saw like the wood-saw Wood saw

would. Now Esau saws wood with that wood-saw he saw saw wood.

Ere her ear hears her err, here ears err here.

I saw Esau kissing Kate. Fact is, we all three saw. I saw Esau, he saw me, And she saw I saw Esau.

Elmer Arnold

I know a boy named Tate, who dined with his girl at eight eight. I'm unable to state what Tate ate at eight eight or what Tate's tête à tête ate at eight eight.

An elephant was asphyxiated in the asphalt.

Elizabeth has eleven elves in her elm tree.

Each Easter Eddie eats eighty Easter eggs.

Extinct insects' instincts, extant insects' instincts.

Excited executioner exercising his excising powers excessively.

I eat eel while you peel eel

Near an ear, a nearer ear, a nearly eerie ear.

Eddie edited it.

Eleven benevolent elephants.

Indy and Iris like to eat ice-cream. They lick it until it melts. Iris also loves to fly kites high up in the sky. Look isn't it nice?

This is Indy the iguana. He drank ink from inkpot in Imelda's igloo. Now he's ill and he needs an injection. Poor little indy!

Can you imagine an imaginary menagerie manager

I correctly recollect Rebecca MacGregor's reckoning.

I eat eel while you peel eel

I scream, you scream, we all scream for ice cream!

I see Isis's icy eyes.

I slit a sheet, a sheet I slit, and on that slitted sheet, I sit.

I slit a sheet, a sheet I slit, upon a slitted sheet I sit.

I slit the sheet and the sheet slit me the slit in the sheet was slit by me

I slit the sheet, the sheet I slit, and on the slitted sheet, I sit.

137

I stood sadly on the silver steps of Burgess's fish sauce shop, mimicking him hiccuping, and wildly welcoming him within.

I thought, I thought of thinking of thanking you.

I was born on a pirate ship - Hold your tongue while saying it.

I wish I were what I was when I wished I were what I am.

I wish to wash my Irish wristwatch.

I wish to wish the wish you wish to wish, but if you wish the wish the witch wishes, I won't wish the wish you wish to wish.

I wish to wish, I dream to dream, I try to try, and I live to live, and I'd die to die, and I cry to cry but I don't know why.

I wish you were a fish in my dish

I would if I could! But I can't, so I won't!

If a bare berry could carry berries?

If a Hottentot taught a Hottentot tot to talk ere the tot could totter, ought the Hottentot tot be taught to say ought or naught or what ought to be taught 'er?

If colored caterpillars could change their colors constantly could they keep their colored coat colored properly?

If Kantie can tie a tie and untie a tie, then why katie may not try to tie the tie to the tree in the theatre.

If Stu chews shoes, should Stu choose the shoes he chews?

If two witches would watch two watches, which witch would watch which watch?

Ike ships ice chips in ice chips ships.

I'll chew and chew until my jaws drop.

Inchworms itching.

Irish wristwatch

Is this your sister's sixth zither, sir?

Impala managing an imaginary menagerie?

Irish wristwatch.

I slit the sheet, the sheet I slit, and on the slitted sheet, I sit.

I thought a thought. But the thought I thought. Was not the thought. I thought I thought.

I see Isis's icy eyes.

Ike ships ice chips in ice chips ships.

Can you imagine an imaginary menagerie manager, managing an imaginary menagerie?

I saw a kitten eating chicken in the kitchen.

I carried the married character over the barrier.

I wish to wish, I dream to dream, I try to try, and I live to live, and I'd die to die, and I cry to cry but I don't know why.

In pine tar is. In oak none is. In mud eels are. In clay none is.

Iranian Uranium.

I would if I could! But I can't, so I won't!

IF IF = THEN THEN THEN = ELSE ELSE ELSE = IF;

Pail of ale aiding ailing Al's travails.

If you understand, say "understand". If you don't understand, say "don't understand". But if you understand and say "don't understand". How do I understand that you understand? Understand?

O

Olive the ostrich and her brother Rob are making corn rolls today. Rob chops the onions. Olive pops the corn rolls in the oven and closes the door. "That won't take long," says Rob.

"Under the mother otter," muttered the other otter.

Awful old Ollie oils oily autos.

Old oily Ollie oils old oily autos.

On a lazy laser raiser lies a laser ray eraser.

One hedgehog hedged up the hedge, whilst another hedgehog hedged down.

Awful old Ollie oils oily autos.

"Under the mother otter," muttered the other otter.

The owner of the Inside Inn, was outside his Inside Inn, with his inside outside his Inside Inn.

One-one was a racehorse. Two-two was one too. One-one won one race. Two-two won one too.

On mules we find two legs behind and two we find before. We stand behind before we find what those behind be for.

Who holds Joe's nose when he blows? Joe knows.

A sad story about Nobody.

This is a story about four people named Everybody, Somebody, Anybody, and Nobody. There was an important job to be done and Everybody was sure that Somebody would do it. Anybody could have done it, but Nobody did it. Somebody got angry about that because it was Everybody's job. Everybody thought Anybody could do it, but Nobody realized that Everybody wouldn't do it. It ended up that Everybody blamed Somebody, when Nobody did, what Anybody could have done.

Polish it in the corner. Polish it in the corner. Polish it in the corner. ...

Red lolly, yellow lolly.

Toy boat, toy boat, toy boat, ...

Mallory's hourly salary.

Octopus ocular optics. And A cat snaps a rat's paxwax.

Nothing is worth thousands of deaths.

How many boards. Could the Mongols hoard. If the Mongol hordes got bored?

Send toast to ten tense stout saints' ten tall tents.

Two-two was one too. One-one won one race. Two-two won one too.

U

Bugsy is a baby bug. This is his mum. Mum has a nap. Bugsy the baby big wants the rug. With a tug here and a tug there he pulls the rug.

Unique New York.

The U.S. twin-screw cruiser.

An undertaker undertook to undertake an undertaking. The undertaking that the undertaker undertook was the hardest undertaking the undertaker ever undertook to undertake.

Plymouth sleuths thwart Luther's slithering.

2 Y's U R. 2 Y's U B. I C U R. 2 Y's 4 me!

Mixed Phrases

Thrushcross Grange.

She sat upon a balcony, inimitably mimicking him hiccuping and amicably welcoming him in.

The Knight said, "He's", with niceties, "some nights a tease or nice at ease on nice settees".

How much snus could a moose on the loose use if a moose on the loose could use loose snus?

Now the trees are all groaning in growling, rough gales That with thuds and hoarse roaring roll raging around! Such leaf-rousing, branch-ruining, ripping, raw wails, Such a terrible, thrashing and tree-wrecking sound!

Corythosaurus bit the gory esophagus of the dilapidated Dilophosaurus who lived in the sorest of forests with the whacky patchy-rinosaurus and the Ceratosaurus, but the poorest and mourish panoplosaurus called Wang sang and rang chorus with the lurdusaurus and the brachiosaurus who was dying of staphylococus- aureas.

"He thrusts his fists against the posts, and still insists he sees the ghosts."

Dimensional analysis

Fuzzy wuzzy: Fuzzy Wuzzy was a bear, Fuzzy Wuzzy had no hair, Fuzzy Wuzzy wasn't very fuzzy, was he?

The foreign authorities put Dorothy in an orange forest.

Yes, she is pure, but so is Mrs. Muir. You're just unsure.

Please do not lure me with your unsure cure.

The leath police dismisseth us, and that sufficeth us.Unique New York, unique New York, unique New York, ...

The king would sing, about a ring that would go ding.

Mares eat oats and do eat oats, but little lambs eat ivy.

Courtney Dworkin

The chief of the Leith police dismisseth us.

So, this is the sushi chef?

A singly circularly linked list.

Hum-min-a, Hum-min-a, Hum-min-a, ...

Really very weary, really very weary, really very weary, ...

Chukotko-Kamchatkan – "pertaining to the Siberian people living in Kamchatka."

Her whole right-hand arm really hurts. Difficult to alarm in Brazil. Come, come, Stay calm, stay calm, No need for alarm, It only hums, It doesn't harm.

A lady sees a pot-mender at work at his barrow in the street. "Are you copper-bottoming 'em, man?" "No, I am aluminiuming them, Mam."

You know New York. You need New York. You know you need unique New York.

Amidst the mists and coldest frosts, With stoutest wrists and loudest boasts, He thrusts his fists against the posts, And still insists he sees the ghosts.

The bottle of perfume that Willy sent was highly displeasing to Millicent. Her thanks were so cold that they quarreled, I'm told her that silly scent Willy sent Millicent.

Yellow butter, purple jelly, red jam, black bread. Spread it thick, say it quick! Yellow butter, purple jelly, red jam, black bread. Spread it thicker, say it quicker! Yellow butter, purple jelly, red jam, black bread. Don't eat with your mouth full!

Argyle Gargoyle

Peggy Babcock, Peggy Babcock, Peggy Babcock, ...

Yally Bally had a jolly golliwog. Feeling folly, Yally Bally Bought his jolly golli' a Dollie made of holly! The golli', feeling jolly, named the holly Dollie, Polly. So Yally Bally's jolly golli's holly Dollie Polly's also jolly!

Out in the pasture the nature watcher watches the catcher. While the catcher watches the pitcher who pitches the balls. Whether the temperature's up or whether the temperature's down, the nature watcher, the catcher and the pitcher are always around. The pitcher pitches, the catcher catches and the watcher watches. So whether the

temperatures rise or whether the temperature falls the nature watcher just watches the catcher who's watching the pitcher who's watching the balls.

Casual clothes are provisional for leisurely trips across Asia.

11 was a racehorse, 22 was 12, 1111 race, 22112. Wunwun was a racehorse, Tutu was one too. Wunwun won one race, Tutu won one too.

Aluminum, linoleum, molybdenum, aluminum, linoleum, molybdenum, aluminum, linoleum, molybdenum...

The owner of the inside inn was inside his inside inn with his inside outside his inside inn.

Brent Spence Bridge. Clay Wade Bailey Bridge. Places in Ohio.

Did Dick Pickens prick his pinkie pickling cheap cling peaches in an inch of Pinch or framing his famed French finch photos?

Rudder valve reversals

the cause of some plane crashes

Birdie birdie in the sky laid a turdie in my eye. If cows could fly I'd have a cow pie in my eye.

Mares eat oats and do eat oats, and little lambs eat ivy. A Kid will eat ivy too, wouldn't we?

The queen in green screamed.

What did you have for breakfast? - rubber balls and liquor! What did you have for lunch? - rubber balls and liquor! What did you have for dinner? - rubber balls and liquor! What do you do when your sister comes home? - rubber balls and liquor!

Denise sees the fleece, Denise sees the fleas. At least Denise could sneeze and feed and freeze the fleas.

Coy knows pseudo-noise codes.

Sheena leads, Sheila needs.

I was born on a pirate ship

One-one was a racehorse.

To sit in solemn silence in a dull, dark dock, In a pestilential prison, with a life-long lock, Awaiting the sensation of a short, sharp shock. From a cheap and choppy chippy chopper on a big black block! A dull, dark dock, a life-long lock. A short, sharp shock, a big black block! To sit in solemn silence in a pestilential prison, and awaiting the sensation. From a cheap and choppy chippy chopper on a big black block!

About Authors

NILAM PATHAK

Nilam is an International Published Author, Management Consultant & Specialized Corporate Trainer in Human Resource Management and Communication Skills. She has worked with leading international brands to support them in enhancing the performance of human resource. She is the director of 'Conversational Skills', a personality development institute, based in India

ANSHUMAN SHARMA

Anshuman is an entrepreneur and investor and has been instrumental in nurturing many successful companies. He has created several profitable companies in various domains. He is also involved in supporting the development of several other organizations. In business, his interests lie in cutting-edge technologies and innovative services.

His guidance has helped many businessmen, investors, and entrepreneurs to succeed in their objectives. He has also supported several entrepreneurship cells and incubation centers.

Made in United States
North Haven, CT
09 November 2021

10949787R00088